BLOOD
THE UNOFFICIAL BIOGRAPHY
JONAH LOMU

Phil Shirley

HarperCollins*Publishers*

HarperCollins*Publishers*
77–85 Fulham Palace Road, London W6 8JB

First published in Great Britain in 1999
by HarperCollins*Publishers*

This edition 1999

1 3 5 7 9 10 8 6 4 2

Copyright © 1999 Phil Shirley

Phil Shirley asserts the moral right to be identified
as the author of this work

A catalogue record for this book
is available from the British Library

ISBN 0 00 274065 6

Printed and bound in Great Britain by
Caledonian International Book Publishing Ltd, Glasgow

BLOOD &
THUNDER

CONTENTS

1 FLIGHT 286

**When you play the All Blacks you are
playing the greatest team in the world,
always.**

David Campese

The big guy was happy. It didn't matter that he couldn't sleep, and he didn't seem to notice the turbulence or the people staring. It was heading towards early evening, the last day of August 1998. North-east Australia drifted by 35,000 feet below as the 747 continued its bumpy ride through a clear winter sky.

Jonah Lomu was eating again, his second meal of the ten-hour flight. Singapore Airlines' fillet of fish with vegetables, no matter how tasty, had not satisfied his hunger so he carbed up on sandwiches and orange juice and in between mouthfuls chatted about his place in the world and life in general, contented right through to his big heart. Every so often he would get up and go for a walk down the aisle and back again, sometimes stopping to chat to other members of the New Zealand Rugby Sevens team, mobilizing his huge muscular frame to ease the symptoms of an illness aggravated by the cabin pressure and long periods of immobility. He can experience sudden dramatic drops in energy levels and has to take aspirin on long flights to avoid blood-clotting.

And yet he was surprisingly upbeat and light-hearted for a man who less than 48 hours earlier had once again defied medical odds to take to the rugby field, only to be the object of much of the harsh criticism levelled at the All Blacks following their final Bledisloe Cup tie against Australia in Sydney. I had watched that game from the comparatively comfortable and yet strangely hostile floor of the Sky City casino in the heart of New Zealand's metropolis; Auckland, the place of Lomu's birth. The gambling floor was packed but, apart from the frenetic Japanese, most people were preoccupied with the action on the giant television screen and there were empty seats at many of the gaming tables. No self-respecting Kiwi wanted to play blackjack or roulette or any other of the games on offer while their beloved but maligned rugby team were attempting to salvage national pride by beating the arch-enemy on their own battleground thousands of miles from home.

As always in this part of the world, expectations were unreasonably high despite an unprecedented losing streak, and Lomu was once again cast in the role of saviour. But it was never going to happen. Fate conspired against the All Blacks and Lomu on that August night, and because defeat is not in the vocabulary of the New Zealand rugby supporter, words failed most people as the screen turned to black: a dark silence just hung there for a while and became a darker whisper that spread from beneath the electric blue lights of the Sky Tower, through the city streets, downtown and beyond. The harbour lights appeared oddly dim, their reflection barely noticeable in the heavy swell of the ocean. Somewhere a flame had been extinguished and the cold wind of failure began to howl and moan, cutting to the bone.

Maybe Lomu felt it too. Inside, hidden from view, the dull-edged knife of disappointment cutting a valley through his soul. But you couldn't tell. Maybe the taste of defeat is less bitter when you've had to swallow the harsh truth of mortality. Lomu, more than most, is aware of life's fragility; against the destruction of his own flesh and blood, loss on the rugby field pales into insignificance, although passion for the game that transformed his life from the gutter to mega-stardom runs deep; deeper than the waters that carried his people from their Pacific island to these shores long before the legend of the All Blacks ever existed.

Since becoming an All Black in 1994 – at the age of 19 the youngest ever – Jonah Lomu, the New Zealand-born son of poor Tongan immigrants, has elevated himself to the dizzy heights of national hero. To many of the 3.5 million inhabitants of New Zealand Lomu is quite simply one of the wonders of their island world. He is up there with the country's other icons such as Sir Edmund Hillary, Sam Neill, Sir Richard Hadlee, Bob Charles, Ernest Rutherford, Dame Kiri Te Kanawa, Sir Peter Blake, Rachael Hunter, Crowded House and Phar Lap. You only have to hear the buzz and feel the electricity surge which comes every time he takes a pass to realize Lomu is the player people put their lives on hold to watch. You only have to hear the hushed excitement and feel the warm glow of adoration which comes every time he walks down a crowded street or gets on a plane to realize he is a genuine star.

Lomu could do almost anything he wanted, and he would never stop being loved by New Zealand. They adore him, because he is an All Black and because he didn't turn his back on his country when the whole world tried to lure him away. After the 1995 Rugby World Cup when Lomu shot to stardom they all came calling: America, armed with fists full of dollars, wanted to cover Jonah in the full glory of the stars and stripes by making him as big as Michael Jordan – Lomu's own idol; England called with the promise of rugby league immortality; Japan came in with filthy rich business deals; South Africa and France too. Lomu could have named his price virtually anywhere on the planet but he chose to stay loyal to the things that matter most to him: his country, his culture, his family and friends, his roots. Of course New Zealand rugby made it worth his while, lining the pockets of the once-penniless product of the poorest area of the country with more money than most people see in a lifetime. But the irony is they needn't have bothered. Jonah Lomu would have stayed for free. He loves being an All Black and being an All Black means living and breathing New Zealand. 'How important is it?' he said, repeating a often asked question. 'I'll tell you how important it is. It's everything, more than life itself.'

Even when he became seriously ill, Lomu couldn't see past the potential consequences for his rugby career. Of course, he thought about other things – such as his wife Tanya, his family, his relationship with God, and all the other soul-deep values that come sharply into focus during times of uncertainty. But during the long days and restless nights of anxiety and fear, he kept thinking about his love for rugby and how, if at all, he could survive without it. 'Being a Kiwi rugby league player is all I ever wanted,' he said. 'Being an All Black is all I ever dreamed of. Staying in New Zealand and earning a good living from doing what I love, it's unbelievable, sometimes I have to pinch myself to make sure I'm not dreaming.'

He is not – but the dream started to fall apart after the 1995 Rugby World Cup and Lomu admitted he was lucky to be sitting on that Singapore-bound plane at all. To have made it through the worst of times, ending up part of the New Zealand Commonwealth Games squad, is remarkable. The fact that he may yet be the man to watch at the 1999 World Cup is a miracle. In the space of four years Lomu's career has come back from the dead. That's why after being involved in the All Blacks' worst losing streak since 1949 Lomu could at least keep things in perspective. After all, a nightmare end to the worst season in New Zealand rugby history, at the Sydney Football Stadium of all places, loses its sting when you've experienced the pain of being told your career is over and your life will never be as good again because of an incurable illness. Of course such words were proved wrong. When New Zealand lost its final Test of a horror 1998 season 14–19 to suffer an embarrassing 3–0 Bledisloe Cup clean sweep at the hands of the Australians – the first time in 69 years it had suffered such an indignation – Lomu immediately remembered the words of his father, Semisi Lomu. 'Jonah,' he said after his son was given the all-clear by medical experts to resume his playing career, 'everything you achieve now is a blessing. God has brought you through for a reason. You must always give thanks.'

And Jonah did, even though his heart felt as heavy as lead when the 29 August defeat in Sydney completed a run of five consecutive Test defeats at the hands of Australia and South Africa to copper-bottom a damning case for filing the All Black team of '98 in the basket marked 'worst of all time'.

In 1949 the All Blacks lost all six matches of their programme, four in South Africa and two in Australia. The mood in New Zealand then had been nowhere near as black as it was when we jetted out of Auckland on that bright Monday afternoon. Most of the rugby sevens squad were just glad to be getting away, especially the All Black players Christian Cullen, Joeli Vidiri and Lomu. The New Zealand public were in an unforgiving frame of mind because for the first time since the middle of this century their team was no longer No. 1. That honour now belongs to the world champions South Africa, and the All Blacks were not even as good as Australia. From first to third-rate losers. Impossible to stomach – unless you've experienced worse.

And so the big white 747 headed west. New Zealand became as small as an emerald glistening on the surface of the vast ocean and Lomu began to think of the future as I attempted to dig up his past. New Zealand coach Gordon Tietjens, a balding, animated man who loves to talk about life, sat opposite me and we both looked at Jonah as he made his way down the plane after sharing a joke with team-mate Eric Rush. 'They seem happy enough,' I said. 'I guess it's a pretty bleak time for New Zealand rugby right now.'

'Yeah, I guess it is,' Tietjens said. 'But having a guy like Jonah around helps. He's such a positive, upbeat guy who by rights shouldn't even be playing the game any more – well, at least that's what some of the medical experts reckon. Some people call him a walking miracle. He's been through a hell of a lot since '95, a hell of a lot.'

18 June 1995, Newlands Rugby Ground, Cape Town, South Africa. This is the date that will live forever in the minds of rugby fans and players the world over. Jonah Lomu,

the 20-year-old new sensation of New Zealand rugby, lined up against England's winger Tony Underwood with a World Cup final place beckoning the winner. A little over 80 minutes later a bewildered, dejected and thoroughly defeated Underwood trudged off the Newlands pitch as a jubilant Lomu celebrated one of the most awesome displays of power, pace and finishing that rugby union has ever witnessed. A star was born, yet his career fell apart almost as quickly as it began. In the following year Lomu's form dipped dramatically and he picked up injury after injury. Then came the shattering news from his doctor that he was suffering from an illness that could prevent him from playing again. The prognosis was bleak. Only an extensive course of drugs and a complete, indefinite rest from rugby could keep it under control and prevent it from getting worse, and even then his chances of ever playing again were slim.

The doctors have told Lomu that his condition will always be with him, but they have it under control and have changed his medication to limit its side-effects. Even so, it's a sobering, sometimes scary, situation for the young Islander. The deformed punching bag at his home in South Auckland is proof of the anger and fear that still occasionally rages in the brave heart of a man who has learned the hard way to live one day at a time. Lomu used to take his frustrations out on the bag after he was diagnosed in the autumn of 1996, especially after one specialist warned that it was touch and go whether he would resume a normal life, let alone play for the All Blacks again. 'The last time I used the punchbag I ripped it off its hinges. That's how frustrated I feel sometimes,' he told his father Semisi back in March 1997.

Then something remarkable happened. Lomu started getting letters from people and places he had never heard of, from as far away and as unlikely as a man in jail in Zimbabwe, urging him not to give up hope. School children sent him letters of encouragement, hundreds and hundreds of people wrote to say, 'Hey Jonah, we're praying for you. Hang in there.' Lomu was deeply touched and from such a heart-warming show of support he gained strength, enough to give him hope.

When he visited Melbourne in 1997 to watch the Bledisloe Cup and cheer on his New Zealand team-mates with more than 90,000 other fans, he was surprised that the Australian players purposely sought him out to wish him well. The same happened when he resumed his international career towards the end of 1997 during the All Blacks' tour of Britain and Ireland. Players from opposing teams were falling over themselves to wish him luck. Everyone connected with the game and even those who are not were thrilled that rugby's biggest star was shining again. 'It was a big encouragement to know that there were so many people out there wishing me well. They'll never know just what their support meant to me. It helped me through.'

He beat the illness, at least mentally, by concentrating on getting better rather than dwelling on his problem. 'In the beginning the disease just freaked me out,' he said. 'I didn't know much about what was happening to me, I couldn't even pronounce half the names of the pills that were given to me to take, let alone the name of the illness. I'm just glad I've got it under control and sorted that out, and I can concentrate on the thing that I love, which is playing rugby.'

Lomu knows the challenges that lie ahead. He is not completely cured yet, nor can he ever be 100 per cent confident of a permanent recovery. The illness that still haunts him and gives him nightmares can sometimes be put into remission, as mercifully appears to be happening with Lomu, but it can also return unexpectedly. If it does he will do what comes naturally to him – fight the battle. Jonah Lomu has never run away from a challenge and there's a look in his eyes that says he never will, even if the odds are stacked against him as they have been for most of his young life. Fate has pulled the mat out from under his feet before but he is still standing.

2 BLACKOUT

I don't care how good a team you are or how competitive, if you lose that sense of enjoyment the rugby itself is not worth the candle.

Gerald Davies, ex Wales and British Lions

The plane suddenly lurched and caught Lomu by surprise. He grabbed hold of the back of a seat for support and was told by one of the flight attendants to sit down. 'Please sir,' she said, 'until the turbulence stops.' Lomu smiled. He is used to riding storms out.

'Can't believe it's him!' The only other guy sitting on my row – the middle section of seats – waved a piece of paper in the air. 'Do you think I could get his autograph? Would he mind?' He shook his head and grinned. 'Jonah Lomu! Who would have thought it?' I nodded and smiled to acknowledge his enthusiasm. He leaned towards me and whispered. 'He doesn't look ill, does he? I mean I've heard it could kill him in the end. Poor fella.'

I felt like saying, 'Get your facts right, buddy,' but I just shrugged my shoulders and listened and in the end I learned something else about Lomu. He inspires the sick and the needy, and the man sitting next to me was one of them. I never found out his name but he had cancer. 'I watched him play on Saturday night,' he continued. 'I know they lost but wasn't he great? You know, every time I watch him play I think, "If Jonah can do it so can I." The doctors tell me I may not live longer than a year and I started to feel sorry for myself. But I'm going to visit my sister in Singapore and I found the strength to do it through watching that man play rugby. The doctors told him he was finished, but hey, what do they know!'

Two days before I left Auckland for Singapore I visited the poor areas of South Auckland, Mangere and Otara, places where Lomu spent his childhood. I also spent a little time in the city and down in the beautiful country town of Pukekohe where Lomu plays his club rugby. In all these places I chatted with people about Jonah. I asked them what they thought of him as a man and a rugby player. Most of them could remember where they were on the day the news of Lomu's illness was broadcast on television and radio, just as people may recall their whereabouts when Princess Diana died or John Kennedy was shot. All of them mentioned the illness and talked about Lomu's remarkable courage. It's the one thing that kept shining through. 'He's an example to us all,' I heard a hundred times or more, and 'He's inspired me to face my problems.' One young Maori couple, in particular, summed up this mood of appreciation. 'Our daughter died of leukaemia recently,' they told me. 'She hated the treatment until one day she met Jonah Lomu at McDonalds. She asked for his autograph and he was wonderful, so kind. We told him she was very poorly and he knelt down and put his hand on her shoulder and said, "Don't be afraid. I am poorly too but together we'll get through it. You'll see." After that she smiled all the way through her treatment and before she died she whispered, "Tell Jonah I did get through it."'

Even before his illness Lomu helped the sick and needy. Not as some kind of image-boosting PR exercise but born out of a genuine desire to ease the pain and suffering of the unfortunate. His own painful experience of 1996 when he ripped knee ligaments, tore a cartilage and several muscles and suffered pinched nerves, taught him it doesn't matter who you are, nobody's invincible. It was during this time that Lomu touched the heart of a nation by taking a seven-year-old girl in his arms to give her the day of her life. They went for a walk in the park and round the rugby stadium. They chatted and laughed together, shared a few burgers, ice cream and jokes. And when it was time for the youngster to go home, she told Jonah she had never enjoyed herself so much. Lomu almost burst into tears because the young girl was not only going home to bed but also to die. She had brain cancer and later passed away but before her young life ended Jonah Lomu gave her a reason to be cheerful, if only for a day. 'I've been lucky to have been given gifts I can use,' he said. 'I feel so humble when I see young children suffering. I realize what I've got and they haven't. I love kids. I want to help.'

It's why Lomu is always ready and willing to go out of his way to do charity work and work with the crippled and the dying. He works with South African president Nelson Mandela to support children's charities and is a regular visitor at the Ronald McDonald House and Starship Hospital in Auckland. He also helps Child Cancer, the Crippled

Children Society and the Kidney Foundation. 'I turn up sometimes just to see how the kids are, see the smiles on their faces. You can get close to some of them. I like to know how they are doing. It's always nice to find some of them have gone home. That's great. Then there's the less fortunate and that's hard. Looking into the eyes of kids who are dying or crippled and seeing how much they want to live or just be normal, yet knowing they are not going to get better. Sometimes it's too much, but I can be strong for them. That's my job, help them fight to stay alive just a little longer.'

I remembered Jonah's words and the words of the young Maori couple who had lost their daughter to leukaemia and I looked at the man sitting next to me who was dying of cancer. He had fallen asleep, clutching his piece of paper. Later during the flight I got Lomu to sign an All Black poster which I gave to the man with cancer. It was the least I could do.

Now our thoughts must turn to rugby, because the reason why Jonah Lomu was on Flight 286 from Auckland to Singapore was to prove, beyond a shadow of a doubt, that he is capable of returning to the kind of devastating form that had made the sporting world catch its breath four years previously. He didn't really want to talk about illness and death or the despair of a nation numbed by the cold smack of a bad losing streak. Lomu wanted to talk about the Commonwealth Games where, he assured me, New Zealand would strike gold. That, Jonah said, could pave the way for an All Black revival and success at the 1999 World Cup finals in the United Kingdom, and anyway he was sick of people saying he is through or that New Zealand are a spent force as a rugby power, as someone had bravely shouted in his face a few weeks earlier.

That particular incident took place after Lomu had emerged from the depths of the King's Park changing rooms at Durban, South Africa in July 1998 when the All Blacks were gloomily contemplating a defeat that shouldn't have been. Their agonizing 23–24 loss to South Africa hurt, especially as the Springboks found an escape hatch, during a frantic final 15 minutes, that should have already been firmly bolted shut. There was pain at the loss and anger too, especially from the humiliated Kiwi fanatics who must be the worst losers in the world.

As a sports writer I could see that some positive steps had been made. With a number of new players on board, the All Blacks had competed against, and perhaps should have beaten, the side which is undoubtedly the hottest property in world rugby at the moment, as they were to prove a week later in the Tri-Nations decider against Australia. This fact was lost on New Zealand fans who even turned on Lomu, usually the last to suffer criticism, although not every All Black has his own Hate Society page on the Internet. On the Saturday night before I joined Lomu and the rest of the New Zealand Commonwealth Games rugby squad on the flight to Singapore, following that frenetic third Bledisloe Cup encounter at the Sydney Football Stadium, the All Blacks were again left to contemplate a win that had got away. But this time, they could take no comfort from any perceived positives. They had again surrendered a match, after confidently building up an 11–0 lead. The result was the defining negative, Australia's 19–14 win handing them their first 3–0 series clean sweep of New Zealand since 1929.

Although it took a 73rd-minute try by Australian fullback Matthew Burke to break the game open, the reality was that the Wallabies should have finished it off far sooner. With a two to one share of second phase and a similar advantage in the ration of penalties from Irish referee David McHugh, which helped to blight the game as a spectacle, the Wallabies should have coasted home. That they didn't was thanks to some stoic defence by the All Blacks, especially in the first half when they effectively shut the Wallabies down, and some bad option-taking. In Burke, winger Ben Tune and gifted first-five Stephen Larkham, who cut the New Zealand defence to ribbons during one stunning piece of individual brilliance in the first half that carried play 70 metres downfield, Australia had three potential match-winners. Tragically for Burke, who was scoring his fourth try in Test matches against New Zealand in the year, he badly dislocated his shoulder in the act of forcing the ball.

It was painful for Burke but even more painful for New Zealand, who had to watch as yet another match got away from them, once Eales had converted to push Australia in front. The Australian captain administered the last rites with a further penalty goal. The agony was over and you should have heard the groans and moans from the floor of the Sky City casino. 'Disappointed' would be the understatement of the year. Individually there were some good points for New Zealanders to mull over: Cullen's class from fullback when given the opportunity, Clarke's powerful running and strong defence, the bounce and enthusiasm of lock Royce Willis and the powerplay of the all-Otago front-row.

But international rugby, as the bartender conceded wearily afterwards, as he passed me another Corona, and more Bourbon and Coke for my choked Kiwi friends, is all about winning. And on that score, for the fifth time in succession in 1998, the All Blacks were dismal failures.

And so it was at last official. In 1998 New Zealand, kings of the rugby world for the last two years, and some would argue three, had been dethroned. In truth they lost their grip on the Bledisloe Cup which they had held since 1995, and any mathematical chance they had of retaining the Tri-Nations trophy which had been their sole property since the competition began in 1996, weeks before Sydney when they lost to Australia at Jade Stadium in Christchurch. Worse than that, however, was that their third consecutive loss in the 1998 Tri-Nations was, without doubt, their most humbling experience of the year. While just four points separated the two teams at the final whistle, two converted tries to the All Blacks in the last five minutes could not hide their deficiencies, or detract from what was a superbly orchestrated victory for the Wallabies.

Up front the Wallabies out-muscled their opponents in an impressive display of driving play built on superior ball retention, their skill best illustrated by a crucial try just before half-time. It came at the end of a memorable movement during which the Wallabies advanced through what seemed like an eternity of passes until just one tackle needed to be missed, and when it was, Matthew Burke scored. It may have been in that moment of Australian brilliance that the end of the All Blacks' reign was finally realized, although their discontent had been sown much earlier.

South Africa's winger Pieter Rossouw had already scored 16 tries in his 17-Test career, including four against France at Paris in 1997, and he hammered another nail in the All Black coffin a month before Jonah Lomu left Sydney vowing to make amends by helping New Zealand win the Commonwealth Games rugby sevens tournament. Rossouw, who would later have something very important to say about

Lomu, admitted that his latest try, which clinched victory against New Zealand at Athletic Park with just ten minutes remaining in the 50th Test of the most intense rivalry in world rugby, was his most important. It was a try which decided a match that until then, the 70th minute, had hung in the balance. It was a try which realistically ended any hopes New Zealand had of defending the Tri-Nations trophy they had held for the past two seasons. It was a try which allowed a Springbok team, winless on the road in the first two Tri-Nations seasons, to go home with two away victories and the real possibility of overall triumph. It was also a try which illustrated why they deserved to win the match. Why? Because their basic execution with the ball – and they had far less of it – was better than the home team's.

The All Blacks with the ball had been unable to break the grip of the Springbok defence. First-five Carlos Spencer missed five penalty goal attempts before being pulled from the game in the 48th minute. His inaccurate goal-kicking was a frustration, but not as galling as the overall malaise of John Hart's side. In attack the All Blacks were quite simply bereft of the ideas, the patience, the fundamental skills and the cohesion to break down a Springbok defence. Basics were missing, like orthodox passing through a well-aligned backline chain, with straight-running midfielders offering their forwards their next target. Targets from which quick second phase could be won; like a drop-out to where the bulk of the forward pack are standing; like playing the game in the opposition's half; like having a simple but effective move to call in try-scoring territory; basics like turning possession into points.

'Basically, unless they learn to make greater use of the attacking gifts of players like Lomu and Cullen, the All Blacks won't get back on their feet,' Rossouw suggested several weeks later. 'Don't they realize that Lomu and Cullen are good enough to win the World Cup for them, if they get decent service? Jonah Lomu must be very frustrated.'

The South African is right. Lomu is frustrated because when he's fully fit and in possession of the ball, he is virtually unstoppable. The All Black backline's ineffectiveness and inability to make greater use of the attacking gifts of the 6ft 5in winger is one of the great mysteries of a season New Zealand rugby won't be allowed to forget. The embers of 1998 continue to burn deep in the broken heart of a proud rugby nation – even Lomu admitted 'some people won't be able to forgive or forget' – and the raking of the coals by the New Zealand Rugby Football Union, John Hart, and his team only served to fan the flames of the common angry belief that the real problem is that the All Blacks have forgotten who they are. The spirit of the legend has got lost somewhere.

Back on the Singapore-bound 747 I asked Lomu, Cullen, Rush and Tietjens for reasons why the New Zealand winter of 1998 had been one of unprecedented discontent. In three months, the All Blacks toppled from an unrivalled ranking as the best in the world to being whipping boys for South Africa and Australia. Thirteen months away from the fourth World Cup, the situation had developed into a national crisis. I learned just how bad it was when the usually brilliant service at the bar and grill I had been using on Queen Street in Auckland suddenly disintegrated. 'Sorry man, but everyone's too gutted to do their jobs properly,' the owner said. 'The chef's completely lost it and I haven't poured a decent beer all night.' As I quizzed Lomu about the plight of the All Blacks I suddenly felt the need to pray that the pilot wasn't a Kiwi.

It was Eric Rush, former All Black, North Harbour captain and New Zealand's Commonwealth Games Sevens skipper, who really started the ball rolling on Flight 286 and it wasn't long after he had finished sharing his thoughts on the All Black crisis that the penny dropped. The fun had gone out of playing for the team. Hart had squeezed the joy out of being an All Black, something that Lomu would admit to before we touched down at Singapore. Rush was sitting alone a few rows back on a window aisle. Tietjens approached him to find out if he wanted to talk. He did, so I ended up spending half an hour with New Zealand's outstanding sevens exponent, a man who can include Lomu and Cullen as two of his biggest fans. Rush didn't even expect to be on the plane. He had been ruled out of Tietjens' plans for the Commonwealth Games after suffering a broken hand in a car crash. But he proved a quick healer and I was grateful for that because of the light he shed on the All Blacks' darkest hour.

'It was never going to be an easy year,' he told me, 'after losing three outstanding players. The heart has been torn out of the team.' Rush is talking about the loss of Zinzan Brooke, Sean Fitzpatrick and Frank Bunce. These are men, legends even, who inspired Lomu to reach for his dream. Brooke opted for the less demanding tempo of club rugby in England; Fitzpatrick's knee caved in; and Bunce was seduced by an offer to end his rugby career in France. 'These three,' Rush said, 'provided immeasurable levels of onfield leadership, inspiration, and tactical knowledge and experience, throughout the nineties. They were never going to be easy to replace.' In the absence of Brooke, Fitzpatrick and Bunce it was accepted, even by Hart, that there would be an inevitable dip in performance while the team regrouped under its new captain Taine Randell. But the dip became a dive and the All Blacks have been out-thought and outmanoeuvred by Australia and South Africa, and if Rush, Cullen and Lomu are to be believed, Hart is largely responsible. 'A number of players feel the team environment is claustrophobic,' Rush added. 'I've heard players complain that the way Hart runs things is not conducive to freedom of expression on the field, and without that the All Blacks cannot function properly. But I'm not the best person to ask because I'm no longer directly involved.'

Rush had said enough, though, and, as Tietjens had pointed out, 'He knows more than most about what's going wrong. Whether he'll talk about it is another matter.' Rush didn't want to say any more so I shook his hand, thanked him for his time and headed down the 747 in search of Cullen.

The shaven-headed 23-year-old fullback first came to prominence in the Hong Kong Sevens, where he became the first player in the event's history to score more than 100 points. Needless to say, the New Zealand team won the event and Cullen would again prove to be arguably the best player, next to Lomu, when Tietjens' Commonwealth Games team attempted to win gold in Kuala Lumpur. But more of that later. Cullen and Lomu, who have become close friends, have two things in common; a love of sevens rugby and Tongan blood. For years people thought Cullen was part Samoan, but in truth he has no Samoan ancestry, just Tongan. His grandmother, Ana, from whom comes his Polynesian heritage, is part Tongan; she has no Samoan blood. She was born in Vava'u, Tonga, close to where Lomu grew up, and moved with her family to Samoa where she grew up. The Cullens then migrated to New Zealand, according to Ana, who now lives in

Timaru. Cullen was actually born in Paraparaumu, the main town of the Kapiti coast area, 34 kilometres north of Wellington in the south of the North Island.

Cullen performs with such natural grace and poise that he threatens to overtake Lomu in the public's affections. Not so long ago, comparing a New Zealand rugby player to a ballet dancer would have invited a broken nose. But the Kiwis' national sport has changed radically since the last World Cup and the manner in which Cullen dances through the opposition has invited comparisons with Mikhail Baryshnikov himself. Under Hart, who took over from Laurie Mains in 1995, the All Blacks are playing an expansive game at the speed of the Super 12 competition. Rule changes have also opened up the game, giving the backs more space to run and more opportunities to score. Cullen's ability to step off either foot at pace makes his play a hallmark of the professional era but, like Baryshnikov, the dancer's allegiance is to his art ahead of his profession. 'It's a passion,' Cullen said in a recent interview. 'To play for the All Blacks – that's the sort of thing you strive for. I mean, it's been a goal of mine since I was a little kid. You get really excited when you pull on the black jersey. Forty thousand people watching you at the ground, it's an awesome feeling. The national anthem settles you down and then you get into the haka and it makes your adrenaline rush ... You just want to get out there and play really well for your country.'

Like Lomu, Cullen is quick to point out that 'sevens is completely different to 15s' but he plays the big game with the same agility which saw him named player of the Hong Kong tournament. Cullen ran in three tries on his debut against Western Samoa and a record-equalling four in his second Test against Scotland, the first of which will remain in many a spectator's mind as one of the most scintillating tries ever. Given the ball within his own 22, Cullen punctured the field with his blistering pace and then waltzed through the Scottish defence, leaving six tacklers hugging thin air in his wake, before scoring under the posts. He's brilliantly balanced, one of those players that picks up pace quickly and runs out of trouble quickly. That's why they call him 'the ghost' – he's there one second and gone the next. Perhaps Cullen's most important trait is being in the right place at the right time but the player is quick to point out that he is playing with two of the best wingers in the world – Jeff Wilson and Lomu. 'When they get the ball all you've got to do is follow them and nine times out of ten you'll end up with a try,' he said. The combination of Cullen, Wilson and Lomu is a potent offensive weapon for the All Blacks. All three are extraordinarily fast and Cullen's vision, Wilson's panache and Lomu's brute strength make them arguably the most gifted back three in world rugby.

Why then have the All Blacks fallen from first to third in the world rankings? Cullen struggled for an answer at first, but then as he thought harder he began to echo the words of Rush and the 'Hart-ache' factor reared its ugly head again. Cullen, an intelligent, sensitive and loyal kind of guy, was reluctant to criticize Hart or the New Zealand Rugby Football Union even though the All Blacks coach had shown no such restraint when defending his position a couple of weeks earlier.

The New Zealand press called for Hart and the NZRFU to examine their demands of man-management and the team's pleas for more room and self-expression. Hart responded by publicly slating the players, venting his anger at the All Blacks' performance, hinting that players had fallen below acceptable standards, talking about some of the finest athletes in the new world of professional rugby as though he were addressing a classroom of naughty children. He wasn't taking the blame or resigning because 'certain people dropped the ball they shouldn't have dropped, threw bad passes, lost the ball when they should have had control. How many times have I told them? I don't know but it's been happening consistently through the year. I'm very disappointed.'

I reminded Cullen of this and asked him if he thought Hart's method of man-management had created a suffocating environment for the players, making it difficult to work. Cullen shrugged. 'Maybe I'm the wrong guy to ask,' he said. 'Maybe you should be talking to Andrew Mehrtens or Carlos Spencer or Josh Kronfeld.' I would have done, but they were not on the plane and were in no mood to talk anyway after the humiliation of Sydney.

But Cullen had a point. How can the performance of consistently brilliant club players like Mehrtens, Spencer, and to a lesser degree Kronfeld, turn into a shadow of that form at Test level? Under Hart, Mehrtens has gone from a happy-go-lucky Crusaders star, who was the commanding player of the Super 12, to what can only be described as an All Black robot who seems to have been drained of his natural exuberance and humour. Spencer has also gone from bright upstart to disorientated lethargic, while the usually fired-up Kronfeld looks just plain extinguished.

While the whole sporting world debated the demise of the All Blacks, Cullen and I sat and watched the world pass by at 35,000 feet, until he said: 'Yeah, maybe you've got a point, perhaps the fun has gone out of playing for the team. But I'm not saying it's all John Hart's fault. He's basically a decent guy and good coach.'

Basically? Whenever someone uses that word you know they're just trying to soften the blow or take the edge off reality. It's the same kind of cover-up as 'take care now' – you know, when you can't wait to see the back of someone. 'Take care ... NOW, because afterwards you'll be taking care of yourself!' So what does 'basically' really mean? It means apart from or despite that or at least. 'He's basically a decent guy when he's not being a complete bastard', or 'she's basically an honest person when she's not lying all the time'.

John Hart is basically a good coach when his team is not losing all the time and a decent guy when he's not being unfair and selfish all the time. Lomu, like Cullen, was reluctant to stick the boot in, verbally, when I wanted to hear the undiluted truth about playing for Hart. 'A lot of things are wrong,' Jonah admitted, 'and some of the players are saying the joy has gone out of playing for the All Blacks.'

'Is it like that for you?' I asked, remembering how dejected he looked before and after the final game of the season against Australia. I also recalled what one of Lomu's team-mates had told me during a phone interview a week earlier. 'Most of us are sick of the way John Hart loves the sound of his own voice. There are times when he won't shut up even though most of us have switched off. He speaks too often and most of the time what he says is too critical, too negative.'

When he was a halfback for Waitemata 25 years ago, Hart had a reputation as a motor-mouth. It seems that nothing has changed and it is now clear that the All Blacks have been subjected to too many meetings. According to the player who I spoke to on the telephone a few days before the Sydney game, several Hart debriefings lasted more than two hours and he harangued the All Blacks in their dressing room for more than an hour after the Melbourne loss to Australia. 'We are tired of listening to John Hart ranting on,' my source said. 'We'd rather take the lashing on the training ground, if we thought we deserved it, but in reality Hart has lost the respect of some of the players.'

Lomu refused to be drawn into that one, but there are other less personal reasons why Hart and the NZRFU must take their fair share of the blame for the All Blacks' fall from grace. Player burn-out is one of them. Not since 1994–95, when Lomu made his debut, have the leading players had a summer off. Such is the intensity of the now professional game that top players are involved almost non-stop from February till December each year. Their bodies are crying out for rest, although, as Lomu pointed out, the All Blacks don't have an overseas tour during the World Cup build-up so the players should be invigorated and ready to fire again, as they were in 1995 for the last World Cup. Hart and the NZRFU have over-whelmed the players by numbers. Hart has gathered too many assistants about him with half a dozen or more assistant coaches, selectors and other hangers-on putting their oar in. The result has been confusion and claustrophobia.

Then there were selection errors, based on that most diffi-cult feeling of loyalty, which eventually told against the All Blacks. Contrary to Hart's assertion at the beginning of the year that he would select on form, he clung defiantly to his old Auckland buddies Michael Jones and Mark Carter, who he considered to be the best players. He was, however, proved wrong, as everyone else in New Zealand and the rest of the rugby world knew. He slammed poor old Mehrtens for his Melbourne performance in the 16–24 defeat to Australia, blaming him for 33 per cent of the mistakes, only to recall him after Spencer missed five goals at Wellington's Athletic Park when the All Blacks lost 13–3 to South Africa. The result? Two halfbacks with shot confidence. Lomu was dropped after the England Test at Eden Park – he still doesn't understand why because Hart never gave a good reason – and Joel Vidiri, Lomu's Manukau team-mate, suffered the same fate after Melbourne.

It all adds up to a major headache for New Zealand rugby and by the time I had walked up and down the 747 a few times, looking for answers amid the dented pride of three All Blacks and the hopes of a dozen other medal contenders as well as digging up the past of a premature legend, my head was also spinning. I felt the same as Lomu. 'Just shut the blinds and let me sleep.'

3 GOLD

**Genius is one per cent inspiration and
ninety-nine per cent perspiration.**

Thomas Edison

Singapore was too hot for pushing and shoving but it was inevitable that as soon as Jonah Lomu set foot outside the Boulevard Hotel he and the rest of us were going to get mobbed. Everywhere this guy goes people, especially kids, go nuts. Unlike Hong Kong, where Lomu is a regular visitor, or South Africa, since the 1995 World Cup, Singapore rarely gets a good look at the man who commands God-like status almost everywhere he goes. Lomu hates all the attention. During their honeymoon in the US Virgin Islands and later at Disneyland, Florida, Lomu and Tanya were mobbed by some Asian tourists. In Auckland it's usually the Japanese who go Lomu hunting, and when he was in London in 1997 a group of tourists from Singapore drove 100 miles to try and get his autograph.

So, Singapore went Lomu crazy during the week Gordon Tietjens and his New Zealand Sevens squad prepared for the

Commonwealth Games, and Lomu probably signed several hundred autographs, before he battled his way to the plane that would eventually take him to Kuala Lumpur and open another colourful chapter in his young life.

Lomu's manager Phil Kingsley-Jones believes, obviously not without bias, that Jonah was destined to be an international mega-star. Normally, I would take with a pinch of salt any such hype from managers or agents, mainly because I haven't met one whose motives are not distorted by self-gratification. Nevertheless, Kingsley-Jones has a point. There is something very special about Jonah Lomu and I am now certain that had he been seduced by an offer to switch codes to American Football, he would have become a celebrity of Jordan-esque proportions. Lomu would probably make an exceptional basketball player, if he put his mind to it; in fact he could have been just about whatever he wanted as a sportsman. At one school athletics meeting he entered the long and triple jumps, hurdles, 100 and 200 metres, discus, javelin and 4x100 metres. He won the lot and only missed out on the pole vault because they could not find one strong enough to support him. The Dallas Cowboys were willing to smash their already outlandish wage structure to secure his unique talent, because they believe what Kingsley-Jones says is true about Lomu: 'He has the magic ingredients for success; charisma, natural ability, sex appeal and guts.' In short Lomu has IT.

But there is something else as well, something that even the screaming fans in Singapore understood; All Black magic. It's the one special ingredient unique to New Zealand rugby and, according to Lomu, accounts for 50 per cent of his pulling power, although it has to be said that Jonah has never really understood what all the fuss has been about since the rugby world became aware of his ability. He is modest to the centre of his formidable physique. 'Being an All Black changes the way people see you,' he says. 'Not only in New Zealand but throughout the world. It makes you feel immortal even though you are not.'

As teenagers New Zealanders learn that rugby union is a potent symbol of their nationhood and by early manhood those who have made the grade are regarded as icons in every town. When a team faces the All Blacks now, in these days of the modern, professional game, they must come to terms with men whose passion has been refined and calibrated by up-to-date technology and focused on a corporate ethic that refuses to acknowledge the possibility of defeat. That's why the failure of the 1998 season was so hard to stomach for John Hart's players, and why, even in the deepest, darkest depths of despair it's been hard for players to speak their minds, no matter how troubled. When a player becomes an All Black it is a bit like joining the mafia: loyalty to the organization is paramount, opponents are there to be destroyed.

But the All Black image has changed, arguably for the better. The 1998 All Blacks confound the myth that Test players have to be giants. Jonah Lomu is the exception that proves the rule. As rugby men go, team-mates such as Christian Cullen, Robin Brooke and Carlos Spencer could easily pass for professional footballers. The great majority of the squad are lean, lithe and well-balanced, on the ground and in the air. New Zealand have also added heart and soul to the intimidating efficiency that has twice taken them to World Cup finals, and this has made each one even more attractive to sports fans.

I bumped into one of John Hart's backroom staff, Mike Banks, on my way to catch Flight 286 from Auckland international airport. He was in a hurry and ended up leaving his briefcase in the luggage compartment on the airport bus, but he still managed to offer this insight into All Black values. 'There has been a major change in the All Blacks' attitude,' he said. 'We do care about people, we certainly care about kids, and when we play our rugby we want people to enjoy what they see. We still want to win all our games but our priority is to play in style and with a smile. We want to look at ourselves in the mirror and be able to say "We did our best on every front".'

The crucial factors that go into the making of an All Black - - pace, balance, hand-eye co-ordination – may be in the genes but men like Hart's assistant coach Ross Cooper, who was a headmaster before he became a professional coach, believes in a structured environment for moulding talent. Becoming an All Black, he suggests, is like enrolling in a unique course of higher education. 'It's essential to have a burning desire to play for your country and to win, but we also believe in the importance of playing fair and providing a role model for younger New Zealanders,' he explains.

'We've always tried to develop an ethos which produces a champion team rather than a team of individual champions. Great old players like Zinzan Brooke, Sean Fitzpatrick and Frank Bunce are only too happy to come and help the young fellows succeed. The key to our tradition is that one All Black never wants to see another All Black fail. We believe our team spirit is unique in professional sport – though the older guys are keen to guard their own jersey, they never want to stand aside and let a new guy come unstuck. I think that's the greatest quality of this team – every newcomer knows he has joined a very exclusive club. We believe All Blacks are All Blacks 24 hours a day every day of the year.'

There is more as well, wider-reaching implications of the All Blacks' overall role. They offer a significant focal point for social and political unity in New Zealand, a country which has had to grapple with increasing demands for Maori self-determination in recent years. 'We are one of two great sporting institutions in New Zealand,' Cooper added, 'the other is the yachting crew that won the America's Cup – and we appreciate the way the nation gets fully behind us whenever we play a Test. We're a small country of just 3.5 million people and we have our struggles but the All Blacks keep going, they are always there. Our vision ultimately is to make the All Blacks' style a world-wide sporting brand that transcends national boundaries.'

The irony of the situation was not lost on Lomu as he trained with the New Zealand Sevens squad at Singapore cricket club. His own personal brand of sporting excellence had successfully transcended another national boundary despite a dramatic downturn in All Black form and marketing value. He would soon be breaking more new ground in ways he could not have imagined two years ago when, weakened by illness, he genuinely believed he was nothing without the mighty All Blacks. His rise to independent mega-stardom has, in many ways, been a process beyond his control. Of course, he, and Kingsley-Jones – as shrewd an agent and manager as you could care to meet – have left nothing to chance, even planning well into the next century the marketing potential of the Lomu brand.

Lomu's genuine deep-rooted modesty, born out of a heritage alien to the act of self-aggrandizement, is at times akin to a pair of blinkers; he can't always see just how powerful he really is, in terms of status in the modern sporting world. But while Hart, despite his recent failings as chief coach, has brought something of his business background to the All Blacks, creating a management team, each of whom has a clearly defined role yet is willing to do things that go beyond that role, and the NZRFU seeks to promote the team globally as a brand alongside Manchester United, the Brazilian soccer team, and the Dallas Cowboys, Lomu has become a separate entity. In many ways he is bigger than the All Blacks.

Longevity has always been very important to the All Blacks: people enjoy playing for the team and staying in the team as long as they can. In the professional era their players continue to have great respect for the jersey and take pride in wearing it. There is no doubt that Lomu takes enormous pride in wearing the No. 11 shirt – remember his All Black philosophy, 'How important is the black jersey? It's life.' But, still, there is no denying that he is no longer only an All Black. Lomu is much more than that and as I watched the awestruck kids waiting for a glimpse of their hero it suddenly hit me – they are not dreaming of becoming an All Black, they are dreaming of being Jonah Lomu.

Back at the cricket club, Tietjens looked like a man who knew something good was about to happen. At the end of another gruelling training session he sat in the sun and squinted at the burning bright light in the Singapore sky. He closed his eyes for a moment, sweat running in fast-moving rivulets down his red face, and saw another bright golden object. It shone like the sun, with more radiance, and he imagined taking hold of it firmly in the palm of his hand and closing his fingers around its precious shape for all time. Lomu had the same vision, so did Cullen, and Vidiri and the rest of the New Zealand Sevens squad. Right now they wanted gold more than anything else life had to offer, and Lomu was the catalyst that, within the space of two weeks, could transform New Zealand rugby from a dark chasm of despair to a shining mountain of hope.

The only cloud on the horizon was Fiji, the undisputed world champions of the sevens game, and, as misfortune would have it, they and New Zealand were on a collision course at the semi-final stage of the first ever Commonwealth Games rugby sevens tournament. Fiji, guided brilliantly by sevens maestro Waisale Servi, claimed the World Cup sevens crown in 1997 and confirmed their status by winning the prestigious Hong Kong tournament in March 1998. That really stuck in Lomu's throat because if there is one thing the big guy loves it's the Hong Kong Sevens. He enjoys it so much he's even got a clause in his contract with the NZRFU which gives him exemption to play in Hong Kong. The Kiwis' sevens captain Eric Rush, who had shed so much light during Flight 286 on the All Black demise, led the team to three titles at the Hong Kong Sevens, where Lomu's rugby career really took off.

There is no doubt at all that the sevens in Hong Kong has been good to Lomu, not just in terms of image-enhancing fan support and the trophies the New Zealand team won, but as a good launching pad for 15's – the full code. 'I find when I come back,' he says, 'I seem to be really firing. The tournament and the place just seems to bring out the best in me. It's a buzz, the whole place buzzes 24 hours a day. It starts when you fly in – that in itself is an experience and a half, flying between all those high-rise buildings. Then there's the speed of the place, thousands of people travelling thousands of miles an hour in thousands of different directions. It's a town that never sleeps – I could never get over that.'

Lomu was only nine when the All Blacks decided to take seven-a-side rugby seriously. That was after the final of the 1984 Hong Kong Sevens, when Fiji took on the All Blacks in a game that produced some of the greatest rugby ever seen. Just before the kick-off, a band of drunken Kiwis in the crowd invaded the pitch and performed a rather poor haka. What followed stunned world rugby. The Fijians glared and, seconds before the start of play, they dropped into a threatening crouch, eyes blazing, and performed their own war dance. You could see real apprehension in the eyes of the All Black players. And then with a roar Fiji were off into a torrent of ferociously uncompromising rugby, flinging the ball across the pitch and plucking it out of the air with overwhelming aggression, confidence and skill. They ran the All Blacks ragged, winning 28–0. After that the All Blacks went back to the drawing board and re-invented sevens and in doing so changed the shape of its future. They became no small representative of brutal, vital force, playing sevens as if it were 15s; running through people instead of round, running faster and harder, turning the ball into a bullet.

Lomu never aspired to be a New Zealand sevens player and his introduction to the specialized code had come as the result of a half-soaked response to an unwelcome late night telephone call five years before. Ross Cooper, the Counties coach at the time, rang Lomu at midnight one evening. Lomu was half asleep and Ross said, 'Hey, Jonah, you wanna play some sevens?' Not entirely with it, Lomu said something like

'Mmm, whatever,' and put the phone down. Ross rang again in the morning and asked if Lomu remembered their conversation. He couldn't remember it at all. That's how he got to his first nationals and he has never looked back.

Lomu loves the sevens game and before the New Zealand squad left their Singapore training camp to compete at the Commonwealth Games in Kuala Lumpur he explained why. 'You get to smash people,' he said, beaming from ear to ear. I wasn't sure if the broad smile was because the thought of sevens violence gave him a kick or whether he was just pleased to have made the final cut for the Games. Lomu's place in the final squad was never really in doubt, although narrowing it down from 16 to 10 was a huge challenge for coach Gordon Tietjens given that his three All Blacks – Cullen, Lomu, and Vidiri – had not played any sevens rugby in 1998. At the back of his mind, however, Tietjens knew he couldn't afford to be at the Games without them, especially Cullen who was the sensation of the Hong Kong Sevens in 1996. Even before we had landed in Singapore, he admitted: 'I can't see us going without them. It won't take Christian long to readjust because he plays his Test match rugby like it's sevens anyway, and Jonah and Joeli will slot back into sevens mode quickly, I know.'

Tietjens was right and the whole of New Zealand, who needed the tonic of Commonwealth medals to ease the pain of All Black failure, was greatly relieved. Having Lomu, particularly, gave the sevens team so many more options. 'He's physically intimidating,' Tietjens added, 'and his mere presence, I know, will worry the Fijians. They couldn't handle him back in 1995 and 1996. He commits so many defenders every time he has the ball. I'm encouraged by what I've seen of Jonah in the Tri-Nations matches. He's trim, obviously extremely fit and seems to have all his old pace back.'

Lomu proved that during training and match practice at Singapore cricket club. He even showed great pace in beating a crowd of autograph hunters to the Boulevard lobby lift doors. 'I'm feeling pretty good,' he said, 'it's the adrenaline, the excitement of taking part in the Games.' I noticed he had his knee taped up during that day's training session. 'Nothing serious I hope.' 'No, just a slight ligament tear,' he replied and slapped his knee with the open palm of one of his big hands. 'I'll be fine, wouldn't miss it for the world. Wild horses couldn't stop me.'

Apart from getting the chance to 'smash people', I reminded him, why else do you love sevens so much? 'With 15s, you haven't got as much room,' he answered, 'you've got less than half the players on the field as well and you get the opportunity to get the ball in hand a bit more. You also get to smash people,' and he grinned again.

Seven months earlier in February 1998, not even the absence of Lomu could stop New Zealand from proving they are now the international front-runners in both 15s and sevens rugby, although now no longer alone as quality exponents of the 15 man game following their Test defeats by Australia and South Africa. The New Zealand passion for anything rugby, though, was so evident during the Sydney Sevens tournament, which ended at Pittwater Rugby Park with the All Blacks easily swatting away Australia in the final. Their almost manic drive to win the 1999 World Cup in Britain has had the New Zealand Rugby Union take the big brother approach – moving contracted players and coaches to whatever area of the country it thinks can help improve the strength of its

BLOOD & THUNDER

provincial structure. And if there was any doubt that New Zealand was as serious in its pursuit to win the Commonwealth Games Sevens gold medal, the NZRFU soon obliterated it, announcing that 20 players, including Lomu and Cullen, had been contracted for the sevens campaign, with the specific aim of winning every sevens tournament around, especially Kuala Lumpur.

The Sydney Sevens victory was New Zealand's fourth tournament success in a month, following triumphs in Argentina, Uruguay and Chile. Their performance during the two-day event, especially their ability to win virtually every kick-off, thus enabling them to hold possession for about 80 per cent of most matches, convinced all they had overtaken Fiji as the trendsetters of sevens rugby. Australia and Fiji were little more than irritants during the lead-up matches, which culminated in New Zealand peaking in the final, scoring six tries almost at will in their 40–5 win. Nothing could distract them – not even a 20-minute power blackout before the final.

And so it came to pass that, despite All Black failure, New Zealand, with Lomu, Cullen and Vidiri on board, as well as the inspirational Eric Rush, were favourites to win gold at the Games. Of course, other genuine medal hopes Australia, South Africa, Fiji and Samoa were also not taking the Commonwealth Games campaign lightly. The brilliant veteran David Campese – widely regarded as one of the greatest rugby players of his generation, holder of the world record for Test match tries, and a member of Australia's World Cup-winning side of 1991 – had been given a brief by the Australian Rugby Union to help sevens coach Tim Lane cultivate a competitive team for Kuala Lumpur, and he was sure Australia would be 'there or thereabouts' when the medals were handed out.

Nevertheless, it would still be hard for Australia to come anywhere near matching New Zealand. Unlike the NZRFU, the Australian Sevens selectors had limited resources, drawing on those who missed Super 12 selection, or were not wanted by Australia for their three World Cup qualifying matches, held shortly after the Commonwealth Games. So Australia headed to Kuala Lumpur with few big names. Campese complained about the selection problems, stating the obvious: 'In New Zealand, they have 20 players contracted for sevens football,' and the less obvious: 'We don't have the depth to do that in Australia, so we have to rely on kids who are not in the top 30 for their province.'

South Africa's selectors muttered something similar, but after talking to Lomu, Cullen and company, the truth of the matter was as plain as the nose on Campese's face. After the humiliation of the All Blacks' worst losing streak since 1949 there was no way New Zealand were going to lose the Commonwealth Games Rugby Sevens; nothing less than gold was acceptable.

Now Campese is a big admirer of Lomu and he knew that as long as Lomu was in form New Zealand would be unstoppable. The pair share a mutual respect, and in many ways Campese has been a distant role model for Jonah. It was the Bledisloe Cup series of 1995 that first gave Lomu the opportunity to face the Aussie legend. He had played Campese at sevens in Hong Kong but it was Lomu's ambition to meet him in Test rugby. Campese, nearing the end of an illustrious career, came on as a replacement for the second half of the Sydney Test. Lomu ended up taking his No. 16 jersey at the end of a compelling 34–23 victory for the All Blacks. Campese, one of the most capped players of all time with 101 appearances for Australia, has never forgotten that moment and it came as no surprise that he couldn't wait to renew acquaintance with Lomu in Kuala Lumpur, even though he knew it would probably involve congratulating him on winning gold for New Zealand.

Not that Campese didn't have faith in his own team, or the ability of world champions Fiji, South Africa or the dangerous Samoans. He did, but his gut instinct, sharpened to deadly accuracy by years of experience, told him Lomu would probably be the star of the show, and if that was the case then New Zealand couldn't really lose. He also felt that Lomu's performance at the Games would be a good sounding board to predict what kind of impact the All Black winger could hope to make at the 1999 World Cup. If Lomu could inspire New Zealand to gold and become the outstanding player of the Commonwealth Games Sevens tournament despite shouldering some of the crushing weight of disappointment and despondency caused by the All Blacks' shocking sequence of results, then surely, when the All Blacks touched down in Britain for the 1999 finals, nothing could stop him from wreaking the kind of havoc that launched his career in 1995. This, Campese suggested, is Lomu's date with destiny.

Ironically, less than a month earlier the Singapore Rugby Union had appointed Campese as assistant national team coach, a major coup for the SRU in their quest to build on their national team's performances and qualify for the 1999 World Cup finals. While hundreds of young Singaporean kids watched starry-eyed as Lomu thundered around the local cricket club Campese was wondering how on earth he could shape their rugby team into a force capable of getting to the place where he knew Lomu and company would be in 12 months' time.

Campese actually led the Australian rugby sevens side to a rare win over New Zealand in the final of the Air France Sevens in Paris in May 1998. It was a timely win less than four months before the sevens game made its Commonwealth Games debut. In the semi-final, the Kiwis beat Fiji 21–19 on the whistle before Campese scored two of Australia's five tries in the final, as his young sevens outfit recovered from a 14–0 deficit to win 33–26. It was the first time New Zealand had fielded a full-strength side at the Paris event, although Lomu, Cullen, and Vidiri were missing through injury and for other reasons. Their return for the Commonwealth Games Sevens meant there would be no repeat glory for Campese's Australia, only a chance for Lomu to execute his plan to perform haka's at each corner of the Kualar Lumpur stadium, after New Zealand had secured gold.

The All Blacks have always excelled in the art of haka, which is the generic term for Maori dance. Henare Teowai of Ngati Porou, an acknowledged master of the art of haka, was asked on his death-bed, 'What is the art of performing haka?' He replied: '*Kia korero te katoa o te tinana*', 'The whole body should speak.' When Lomu is doing the haka it's usually before a game, the issuing of a challenge to the opposition, but if New Zealand won gold at the Commonwealth Games, Lomu wanted to leave a lasting impression on the watching world. A haka to restore pride and put fear back into the hearts of those who doubted All Black power. It would be a powerful message of defiance and of course celebration.

The haka is a composition played by many instruments. Hands, feet, legs, body, voice, tongue and eyes all play their part in blending together to convey in their fullness the challenge, welcome, exultation, defiance or contempt of the words. Lomu, like most All Blacks, has spent hours getting it right. It is disciplined, yet emotional. More than any other aspect of Maori culture, this complex dance is an expression of the passion, vigour and identity of the race. It is, at its best, truly, a message of the soul expressed by words and posture. There are several styles of haka. *Ka Mate* was originally of the *ngeri* style, which is a short, free-form haka where the performers interpret as they feel fit. It is also performed without weapons, and is not therefore a war-dance as is generally supposed. The *peruperu* is a style of haka for true war-dance. It involves weapons and is characterized by a high jump with legs folded under at the end. Observers of the All Blacks will note that they perform this same jump, which is a point of irritation amongst haka purists. In fact the All Black rendition of Ka Mate may have undergone quite a few changes along the way to make it more impressive.

A few years ago, around 1995 or 1996, the All Blacks' famous haka ruffled the feathers of sections of the very Maori community from where it originated. The then New Zealand Maori rugby coach Matt Te Pou said the Ka Mate version of the haka used by the All Blacks was identified with the nineteenth-century warrior chief, Te Rauparaha, who slaughtered South Island Maoris during several forays south. 'He decimated the local Maori down there,' Te Pou said. The haka performance itself, which overseas is more well-known than the New Zealand national anthem, was too important to dispense with so it nevertheless remained.

As far as rugby is concerned the first haka in an overseas representative match was performed by the New Zealand

Native Team which toured the UK in 1888–89. It isn't clear whether or not it was Ka Mate which they performed, but it is probable. At many venues they went to some trouble to entertain, bringing out mats and other items onto the field to complement the performance. In fact this team was not entirely composed of Maori, as many assume. The tour was not officially sanctioned, and cost each player the large sum of £250 passage. This made it impossible to find the required number of Maori, and at least two 'dark-skinned' pakeha (i.e. white New Zealanders) were included. The first use of the haka by the All Blacks was by the 'Originals' in 1905 on the first overseas tour by a full-scale New Zealand representative side. It was also on this tour that the name 'All Blacks' was first used. The two most distinctive features of the New Zealand team were thus instigated right from the very beginning. The haka became a permanent fixture for the All Blacks from then on.

One famous anecdote is told regarding the 1924 New Zealand team which became known as the famous 'Invincibles', due to their winning every match on tour. This team had as their most famous son, a young Maori boy called George Nepia. He it was who led the All Black haka, Ka Mate, in the first match against Devon on 13 September 1924. The haka was enthusiastically received by the crowd of 18,000, who then watched the All Blacks win 11–0, but a 'prominent university sportsman' who attended was moved to write a letter which appeared in the next day's paper. In it he asserted: 'Cat-calls were quite uncalled-for', and added: 'South Africans do not open their games with Zulu cries!' Obviously, this gentleman had never visited either country.

The words of Ka Mate, do not have direct relevance to rugby and in the case of the All Blacks the 'loose' translation of the haka challenge is: *'We are the All Blacks, of the New Zealand people. Here we are to face you. We will do you the honour of playing to the limits that our hearts and sinews impose upon us. We will be very hard to beat.'*

In the end they proved impossible to beat. Campese's prediction came true when New Zealand's 100th gold medal in Commonwealth Games history was won by Tietjens' outstanding team. In the opening match they beat Sri Lanka 80–0, running in 12 tries. The half-time score was 42–0. And in the second game against Malaysia the team ran in another nine tries in a 59–0 win. New Zealand almost hit the 100 points mark in their third match, against the Bahamas; instead they had to settle for 93–0. That result followed a much harder-fought match against Tonga, when the Kiwis went 12–0 down and trailed at half-time before running out comfortable winners by 41–12. Wales battled hard but crumbled 38–14 in the quarter-finals. Samoa fought harder in the semi-finals but New Zealand would not lie down and came back from a 7–0 half-time deficit to win 19–14. The mighty Fijian team threatened to spoil the inevitable Kiwi party but, as Tietjens had predicted weeks earlier during that bumpy ride on Flight 286, the world champions couldn't handle Lomu and New Zealand won 21–12.

In total New Zealand scored 351 points – an average of almost 50 points a game – and ran in over 50 tries. Lomu, a name that first surfaced in the game of sevens rugby, was the star of the tournament. Even Cullen, who played out of his skin, couldn't touch him. Lomu's defence was devastating, his attack breathtaking; power, finesse, skill, he possessed all and much more. Pure gold. He shed tears of joy as the New Zealand team completed their lap of honour, stopping at the centre of each stand and performing hakas to the adoring crowd. 'We are the All Blacks,' Lomu cried, and with each shout he raised their spirit out of despair as if to prove to the whole world that while there is strength in his body All Black power will never die.

4 NATIVE LAND

**Not Chaos-like together crush'd and bruis'd,
but as the world harmoniously confus'd,
where order in variety we see,
and where tho' all things differ, all agree.**

Alexander Pope

It felt like the edge of the world. It was the edge of the world. A million miles from home and a million miles from the heart of the city where Jonah Lomu's black-clad giant of a body and clenched face is immortalized in almost every imaginable way; on the side of buildings, bottles and books, phone-cards, T-shirts and computer screens. The legend there for all to see and buy, for a price. I had to get away, if only for a short while. It mattered to me to feel free; loosed from the chains of the city, somewhere where I could breathe again. I wanted to forget about Auckland and Sky City where the weight of Lomu's past and the All Blacks' failure oppressed. So I left Auckland behind, watching the Sky Tower shrink in the rear view mirror, and headed out to the ocean.

In truth I wasn't going far, 40 or 50 miles south-west of the city where the Waikato River spills out into the Tasman Sea, but it was far enough. The waters of the Waikato stretched out before me as I crouched on the sand. My reflection was broken and muddy in a pool left behind by the turning tide and I closed my eyes and listened to the sound of silence. Now and then the wind picked up and whistled, the river stirred and the dunes whispered, but silence would not tolerate the interruption and it hushed the noise into submission as quickly as it had begun. Here in this place of natural beauty, silence is a balm; peaceful healing. It closes the gap between earth and heaven, joins the sea and sky. It makes all one with creation and the wisdom of the age is replaced with faith in the source of all life. I realized why Lomu loves this place so much, why he sometimes drives to the ocean and listens. What are you listening for? The power of the ocean and the speed of the wind? The hush before the storm, rain and the slow turning of the earth? The language of the land?

It is not hard to understand why New Zealanders have such a strong attachment to their native land. It is a place of unrivalled beauty. A land of majestic snow-capped peaks and unexplored rain forest, of unspoilt lakes teeming with life, of glaciers and fiords, geysers and volcanoes. It is a land where oceans of the purest, deepest blue water are speckled with the greenest wooded isles, of kauri forests and rolling hills. It is the land of the Maori, the indigenous Polynesian inhabitants who have made these islands their home for more than 12 centuries.

According to history the Maori came to these islands by outrigger canoe in the 8th century AD. Maori legend tells a very different story, about the birth of all life in the stillness of a long, dark night, Te Po, from the primordial parents – Rangi-nui, the Sky Father, and Papa-tu-a-nuku, the Earth Mother, a passionate pair who refused to stir from their tight embrace leaving their children to squirm and almost suffocate between their clasped bodies for an eternity. Tane, the god of the forests and their eldest son, pulled himself free of his parents in the darkness and with great effort, over a long period of time, pushed them apart. He lifted Rangi into the sky, making sure to cover his nakedness with the sun, moon and a great mantle of stars. To clothe his mother Papa, Tane joined with the elements to create many trees and lakes, which he strewed across her vast expanses. She was covered with plant and animal life, flooding this new universe with light and colour. But Rangi's sorrow at the parting from his mate caused tears to flood from his eyes, filling her surface with oceans and lakes. As a result, the sky and the earth remain separated today, so that life can find its place between.

Human life found its source in yet another divine son, Tiki, who desired to become the father of all humankind. He consulted with the wise river Wai-matu-hirangi and decided to form a human figure out of sacred red sand and chanted a *karakia* – ritual incantation – to create Marikoriko, the first woman. According to some versions of the myth, it was one of Tiki and Marikoriko's sons, Te-a-io-whaka-tangata, who went on to father the Maori people. The land was then created when another son of heaven and earth, Maui, hauled up an enormous fish out of the sea that turned into the North Island, while his boat and anchor weight became the South Island and Stewart Island.

As legend has it, the Maori forebears had been living happily for many years in Hawaiki, the ancestral homeland, when Kupe the explorer set out on a scouting expedition to the east. He discovered a lush, mist-covered stretch of land which he named Aotearoa, 'the land of the long white cloud'. Years later, when intertribal war finally forced the ancestors to leave Hawaiki, they remembered Kupe's praise of the land to the east, and in seven giant canoes the ancestors turned their backs on Hawaiki and set sail for Aotearoa.

The origins of New Zealand and its people are tangled roots of mythology and science, clashing and conjoining as they search for the source of life and the universe. The non-Polynesian influence of men like Abel Tasman, the Dutchman who discovered the South Island in 1642, and the legendary British explorer Captain James Cook, who sailed into her golden shores on the *Endeavour* over 100 years later, add spice to New Zealand's intriguing origins. It's easy to fall in love with all this. It's easy to allow one's heart to melt into the paradisaical harmony of the 'land of the long white cloud'. Impossible to resist.

I remembered the words of Ted Hughes in *Tales from Ovid*, and how God sorted out chaos. How he

rolled earth into a ball and commanded the water to spread out flat, to lift itself into waves according to the whim of the wind, and to hurl itself at the land's edges. He conjured springs to rise and be manifest, deep and gloomy ponds, flashing delicious lakes. He educated headstrong electrifying rivers to observe their banks – and to pour part of their delight into earth's dark and to donate the reminder to ocean swelling the uproar on shores. Then he instructed the plains how to roll sweetly to the horizon. He directed the valleys to go deep and the mountains to rear up humping their backs. Everywhere he taught the tree its leaf.

You listen but the only sound you hear is the beating of your own heart. The pumping of blood. The rhythm of mortality. The silence of nature cannot hush it; the immensity of space and time cannot hide it. Lomu has learned to listen. He's taught himself to meditate, to be in touch with nature. The five years he spent in his native Tonga as a young child made him appreciate the beauty of creation. Ever since he has had a desire for space, to be free from the city and the suburbs, but there was a time when he lost sight of the things that are most important to him and it wasn't until the fragility of his own mortality undermined his strength, like a fissure in rock, that Lomu renewed his faith in the source of life.

Sometimes Lomu drives out to the ocean or the mountains, closes his eyes, and thinks about God and creation and his own place in the universe. Sometimes he only goes as far as the edge of the small lake in the grounds of his house and sits, legs crossed and eyes closed, listening to the movement of water and the gentle stir of wind in the grass and trees, feeling the cool breeze on his face and the earth close to his body. This oneness with nature has been part of Lomu's healing from the disease that brought the man-mountain to his knees. Love has been part of his healing, because without his wife Tanya, Lomu could have crumbled. God has been part of his healing and so has rugby, his other true love. But nature has played a vital role. Nature and the space of the countryside. Like the Maori, Tongans possess an innate, even spiritual, need to bond with nature. Their migration may lack the ethereal romance of the epic canoe journeys across the Pacific of the Maori over 1,000 years ago, but Tongans have their own magical place in this irresistible melting pot of humanity, and the threads of their ancient culture form a rich tapestry as enchanting as the mythical origins of the Maori.

The Maori formed the first great Polynesian migration to New Zealand; Tongans were included in the second wave, leaving the homelands that were scattered across the Pacific from their island in the west to the Cook Islands in the east. This second migration had its small beginnings when Pacific Islanders, including direct descendants of Jonah Lomu, were brought to New Zealand for training by missionaries. After World War II the Islanders came in to fill labour shortages in New Zealand's industrial expansion. Once settled, they brought in their families, forming links that extend into every village on every Pacific island from Tonga to the Cook Islands. That is how Jonah Lomu's mother and father, Hepi and Semisi, came to settle in South Auckland, and they came fuelled with the same expectations that sustained the Maori during their journey to the promised land. 'You will have space, beautiful space to live your lives,' they were told as they watched Tonga fade into the vast Pacific distance, and so from father to son a desire to put down roots deep into the New Zealand earth was born.

Jonah Lomu was born an ocean apart from the island paradise where his mother and father and their parents grew up, but he returned to Tonga at the age of one and was changed forever. From the moment Semisi Lomu introduced his young child to the crystal blueness of the Pacific and the waves washed over their bare feet, Jonah Lomu could never feel at home in the city. The boundless world around him stole his heart and shaped desire and reason, forming a special link with all the natural magic of the sacred red sand from which Tiki conjured up life so many, many years before.

Semisi and Hepi used to tell Jonah the Tongan story of creation. He would sit on his mother's lap and listen to the tale of how the land of his forefathers came into being. It's a story he heard many times and he'll tell it to his own children one day, if things work out that way, even though their myth of creation is based on an incestuous relationship between brother and sister and is far removed from the reality of Lomu's own belief in creation.

Young Tongan children are told that in the beginning there was just the sea and the spirit world, Pulotu; and between them was a rock called Touia'o Futuna. On the rock lived Biki and his twin sister, Kele, 'Atungaki and his twin sister, Maimoa'o Longona, Fonua'uta and his twin sister, Lupe. Biki lay with his own sister and she bore him two children, a son, Taufulifonua, and a daughter, Havea Lolofonua; 'Atungaki also lay with his sister and she bore him a daughter, Velesi'i. When Taufulifonua grew to manhood, his sister, Havea Lolofonua, bore him a son, Hikule'o, Fonua'uta lay with his sister Lupe, and she bore him a daughter, Velelahi. Velelahi bore him a son, Tangaloa, and Velesi'i bore him a son, Maui. Hikule'o, Tangaloa and Maui divided the creation between them. Hikule'o took as his portion Pulotu, Tangaloa took the sky and Maui the underworld. Hemoana, whose form was a sea snake, and Lupe, whose form was a dove, then divided the remainder between them, Hemoana taking the sea and Lupe taking the land.

Tangaloa had several sons in the sky: Tangaloa Tamapo'uli' Alamafoa, Tangaloa 'Eitumatupu'a, Tangaloa'Atulongolongo and Tangaloa Tufunga. Old Tangaloa grew tired of looking down from the sky and seeing nothing but sea, so he sent down Tangaloa'Atulongolongo in the form of a plover to see if he could find land. All Tangaloa'Atulongolongo could find was a reef below the water, where 'Ata is now. So Old Tangaloa told Tangaloa Tufunga to throw down into the sea the chips from the wood carving on which he was working. Tangaloa Tufunga continued to do this for a long time, and on two occasions Tangaloa'Atulongolongo flew down in the form of a plover to see if anything had happened, but found nothing. On the third occasion, however, he found that the chips had formed an island. This was 'Eua. Later, Tangaloa Tufunga threw down more chips to form the islands of Kao and Tofua.

Tongatapu and most of the other islands were the work of Maui. One day Maui visited Manu'a and there an old man, Tonga Fusifonua, gave him a fish-hook. Maui went fishing with this hook, but when he tried to pull in his line he found it was caught. He exerted all his strength and succeeded in hauling the line in, to find that he had dragged up Tongatapu from the bottom of the sea. Maui continued fishing with this wonderful hook and so pulled up from the deeps the rest of the islands of Tonga, and some of those of Fiji and Samoa as well.

'Ata began as a reef below the water and slowly rose out of the sea. One day Tangaloa'Atulongolongo visited 'Ata in the form of a plover and dropped a seed from his beak upon the island. The next time he visited 'Ata he found that the seed had grown into a creeper until it split in two. Then he returned to the sky. A few days later he returned to find that the root had rotted and a fat, juicy worm was curled up in it.

He pecked the worm in two. From the top section a man was formed called Kohai. The bottom section also turned into a man called Koau. Then the plover felt a morsel left on his beak; he shook it off and it turned into a man called Momo. Kohai, Koau and Momo were the first men in Tonga. Maui brought them wives from Pulotu and they became the ancestors of the Tongan people.

'Tonga, its history and culture, its soul and spirit, runs deep in me, like still waters,' Lomu said. 'I could never be happy pretending otherwise. You can't escape your roots. It's like a calling. I'll never forget my early life in Tonga. It shaped who I am. The main reason why Tanya and I chose to live away from the city is because we both wanted space, lots of space. I wanted to live out in the countryside, I need the freedom and the privacy of spending my days in a place that is wide open and not crowded. Maybe it comes from the years I spent as a child in Tonga where you cannot help but be one with nature. Tonga is such a beautiful place.

'My roots are there and the reason why I love nature so much. I drifted away from the things that are most important to me now, like appreciating the planet we live on, and God. Sometimes I look at the ocean or the stars in the night sky and marvel at the way everything is put together. I'm lucky I live in a place where beauty is all around me. I love where we live. Being here makes me feel alive.'

Jonah and Tanya chose to live on the breathtaking Karaka Park Estate in Karaka, South Auckland. Tanya found the house after months of searching. It was love at first sight. It was also perfect for Jonah because he wanted to stay in South Auckland, within reasonable driving distance of his parents' home in Mangere and the idyllic township of Pukekohe where he plays his club rugby for Counties Manukau. Compared to the Lomu family home in Mangere and his early childhood home in Tonga the Karaka Park Estate property may as well be on another planet. It's a palatial paradise. Perfectly designed architecture, made for the man who has money to burn. The Mangere home, a painfully modest small wooden house, would probably squeeze into the middle section of the 6,000 square foot Karaka mansion. Lomu is living like a king after reaping the rewards of a whirlwind leap to the top of his sport while his parents and younger brother inhabit a world of comparative poverty in the poorest area of South Auckland. Lomu is rich enough to put them into a Karaka Park mansion of their own, but that is unlikely to happen because of the strong Tongan culture and family values that dictate the life patterns and roles of members of the extended family. Jonah Lomu has almost everything now, but living in a $3 million dream house with majestic arches, Italian styling, and salubrious surroundings hasn't changed him so much as to separate him from his roots. It's easy to say and just about every successful star that ever lived has at one time or another claimed indifference to material wealth. Not many are sincere – but Lomu seems to be.

His goal when he left school was to have his own roof over his head within five years, which under the circumstances of his past existence is no mean ambition. Many young Polynesian guys looking for a better way of life after growing up within the often desperately frustrating confines of the poor and sometimes violent streets of South Auckland never get what most of us take for granted. For Lomu, after being born in semi-poverty amid the impoverished suburbs of Manukau and spending the next five years of his life shoeless in a Tongan shanty, buying or renting a property, no matter how basic, anywhere in the shadow of the North Island metropolis was a dream barely within reach.

In the New Zealand winter of 1998, with the money rolling in from fresh sponsorship deals and the Karaka mansion looking more opulent than ever before, Lomu considered his position. He'd missed the family reunion at 8a Maitland Place, Mangere, where members of the extended family from as far afield as America crammed into the humble green and white wooden house and celebrated for days, drinking beer and wine and feasting on smoked pig, chop suey and mussels. The rugby Test in Australia had prevented him from returning to Mangere, nothing more sinister. There were suggestions that Lomu had wanted to stay away, in the same way that he had snubbed his parents by marrying his wife Tanya in secret, but it isn't true.

'I love my family,' he said. 'My heritage is very important to me and my success has not changed the way I feel about where I came from or who I am. I have got a lifestyle that I never dreamed I'd have. My goal was to have my own roof over my head by my early twenties. I achieved that goal much earlier. I would be a liar if I said my success has not changed my life. It has because I am now rich and money buys freedom, creates opportunity that would otherwise be denied. The success has changed the way I live, but inside I am still the same Jonah Lomu.

'People may not believe me when I say this, but I would still be happy and contented if I was not a successful man. Wealth is not important to me. Money has made me comfortable, provided nice things, given Tanya and me security and a good future, but what really counts is spiritual contentment and peace of mind. My parents are very happy, the people in my old neighbourhood are very happy. They haven't got much in terms of material wealth but what they lack there they make up for in riches of the soul. It's a hard culture for people to understand.'

Although Tonga's written history is relatively recent, a rich oral history and artefacts here and there have allowed historians to build pictures or interpretations of life prior to white contact. The colonization of the Tonga Islands occurred about 3,500 years ago. The origins of these settlers is unknown. Botanical records, food production, language and material artefacts imply immigration from the west and some believe that pre-European colonizers of the islands of Tonga, Samoa and some migrants to Fiji were from the same seafaring people. It is uncertain, and widely debated on the islands, whether these immigrants originated from Micronesia, or whether they have more exotic origins. Arriving on large dual-hull vessels, the new settlers sustained themselves through fishing (probably on smaller out-riggers). Initial existence was primarily dependent on the sea and tools were made from shell and stones. Nets were made and cast, the stars were studied or reviewed for their navigational properties along with their mystical powers. In time, the imported plants bore fruition in the form of the coconut, taro, breadfruit, yam, banana, and meat such as rat, pig, dog and fowl. While the men tended to life from the sea, it was up to the women to break and tame the land for the garden.

There was no refrigeration, so what the seafarer caught in abundance, and what the farmhand reaped, was readily shared with neighbours. The settlers over time lost contact with their origins and their compatriots in Samoa and Fiji. Traditional handicrafts that thrived in the new environment were continued, such as fishing, while others were substituted by more relevant crafts. Clay pottery was replaced by more expedient, production-effective woodwork. New skills such as farming seem to have been developed to complement the takings from the sea. When the settlers again felt the urge to rediscover lost lands, contact was resumed with the descendants of those who had migrated to the Samoas. Some descendants of the Lomu family still live in the Samoas.

Distant family members were among the seafarers and fishermen who built their homes around the coast and the farmers moved further inland finding the easy, fertile soil. Villages and townships did not exist as the land and its fruits were plentiful. There were relatively few specialists, such as navigators or house builders, and the population seems to have been satisfied with its existence. Excess food could not be hoarded so there were few inhibitions to the sharing of basic necessities. Currency was irrelevant and the bureaucracies to support a currency-based economy did not exist. If a grower's production was low they gladly accepted their neighbour's surplus. Likewise, a grower's surplus was readily shared with neighbours. The Tongan community in South Auckland sticks to these principles even now, in the largely self-preserving society of the modern world. When I was in Mangere I saw families helping out fellow Tongans who were perhaps struggling to make ends meet. The sharing of surplus goods continues. There is harmony, although Tongan history has had its share of trouble.

Social interactions between groups included many internal wars as the population grew, and the possibility of gathering together against the gods and nature required some observance of a system of governance. An elite class – *hou'eiki* – ruled over districts which were subdivided to a middle management group – chiefs/*mu'a* – who sublet these land holdings to the common folk or slaves – tu'a/*hopoate*. It is not certain that all Tongans accepted this mechanical directioning of life.

Tongans developed a complex family ranking system whereby the eldest female, and her descendants, held higher rank within the family than the brothers. This seemingly unique maternal structure intertwines with the paternal inheritance system – the eldest son receives rights to all property and titles – to develop a system whereby no two individuals can hold the same rank within society. For example, individual A may have higher paternal or social rank than individual B, but is inferior to B if B's mother is the eldest female in the family of A's father. In the case of the Lomu family, the ranks and ties are so complicated that even Jonah struggles to explain how it works.

He said: 'It's extended family orientated. You don't just stop with your parents, or even your aunts or uncles. It goes way past that. I still see all my Tongan friends, good friends from my school days. I may be living a different life now but I know where I belong. A great friend is my cousin Henry. I've always hung out with him, ever since I was little. It's been harder since I became an All Black because of the touring, but if I was ever in trouble I'd always go and see him. When I needed someone to talk to, he was always there.'

Henry, an elusive, easy-going kind of guy, won't talk about his relationship with Lomu. It's probably a consequence of the pakeha syndrome. Pakeha is the name given to Europeans by the Maori although most Pacific Islanders – Tongans, Samoans, Cook Islanders – almost always refer to 'white folk' as palangi. Henry, like many of the Tongan people I met in Mangere, is suspicious of palangi, but there are exceptions to the rule.

Pau is one of them. He was born in Tonga, but moved to Auckland as a young boy and lives with his wife Mellie and several children next door to Lomu's parents. Pau remembers playing cricket in the Maitland Place cul-de-sac with Jonah Lomu. Had Jonah not become the success he is today he would probably still be there, living with his parents and younger brother and joining in a game or two. I was a guest of Pau and Mellie for two days and I joined in a game of cricket outside the Lomu family home with Pau, Jonah's young brother, and a number of other Tongan guys. Some looked me up and down with suspicion in their eyes but Pau wanted to talk. His grasp of English is limited but he tried really hard and, with the help of a $20 interpreter, I learned more about Lomu's way of life before his meteoric rise to superstardom from Pau than from Jonah himself. Sometimes it's easier to be objective when you are on the outside looking in.

Pau is a bit player in the Jonah Lomu story, but he is what Lomu could have been, and that's not being disrespectful because Pau is one of the most decent guys I have ever met. He feels the same things as Lomu because they share a past, and the same values that enable the millionaire All Black to keep his feet on the ground and stay in touch with his roots.

Pau offers a rare insight into Lomu's psyche. He also explains, better than most, about the memories that inspire Lomu's 'sense of place' – the place where Lomu belongs, spiritually, and the reason why he often feels the need to be alone with nature, whether it's sitting on the wooden deck by the small lake in his garden or looking out across mountains and oceans. 'It's about keeping one's sense of place, spiritually and physically, in changing times,' he says. 'There have been many changes in Jonah's life. A lot has happened to him in a short space of time. It's easy to lose your sense of place when changes happen. Tongan people place a lot of emphasis on a sense of belonging. Belonging to our culture, to our family, the community in which we live. Belonging to God and belonging to the planet on which we live.

'There is a sense in which nothing ever changes except change itself. In this modern world people strive for change. There is nothing wrong with change as long as your peace of mind remains even when there is no change. You will find with many Tongans that they are happy to stay in one place doing the same thing without feeling bored or restless. By and large Tongan people have a genuine sense of contentment. I believe Jonah is sincere when he says he is not interested in success and riches alone. It was not that long ago when he was living here in Mangere and he comes back often. He loves this place, as much as he loves Tonga, and he visits there as often as he can.'

Pau says that one of the main reasons why Lomu chose to stay in South Auckland instead of accepting offers to play rugby in England or American football in the United States is his need to stay close to the things that really matter to him. 'I think Jonah feared what may happen if he left,' Pau said. 'So much can change in a short space of time when there is distance between a man and his roots. We can easily lose our *Tuakiri* – our sense of belonging.'

Lomu certainly has a positive interest in the cultures of his birthplace and the place where he spent five years of his young life before he returned to South Auckland at the age of six. He has donated large sums of money to help community projects in Manukau and Tonga. He could easily slip back into the Mangere way of life because he has a sense of place and a feeling of being proud still to belong. 'Money alone is not the sole measure of achievement,' he told me. 'Different people have different needs and values to be happy. Pride and belief in who you are is more important than success, although pride and belief in myself helped me get where I am today. I am very proud of my background. Proud of my family and my people.'

The distinctiveness of the Tongan community in New Zealand was defined back in the 1950s when Queen Salote founded the Tongan Society in Auckland, to bring people together and organize social functions. Tongans have since spread around the country, even as far away as Christchurch and Dunedin in the South Island. The Church has been the major meeting point in the dispersal, particularly the Wesleyan, Free Tongan and United Churches. Here Tongans have divided where possible into the same village groups as those back home. Mangere is a case in point. Lomu's parents and members of their extended family attend a Wesleyan church which resembles a slice of Tonga right in the heart of South Auckland's sprawling Polynesian suburbs. When Lomu was growing up in Mangere he went to church every week. He was made to, but it is largely within their church congregations that Tongans retain their language and identity, and for Lomu it was a positive experience, that and feeling the island earth between his toes. Lomu learned how to crawl, walk and run in Tonga but he learned how to pray and believe in the 'source of life' in Mangere.

Lomu is not an orthodox Christian. He rarely attends church, mainly because of his hectic globetrotting lifestyle. He prays and reads the Bible, regularly, but he rejects the inevitable 'born-again' label so conveniently attached to him by the media. Unlike his former All Black team-mate Michael Jones, now retired from the international game, Lomu doesn't have a problem with playing on Sunday. 'I don't feel the Lord is saying, "Don't play on a Sunday Jonah," and I have prayed about it,' he says. 'Religion plays a big part in my life, especially over the last year or so when I have had to deal with my illness. I'd drifted away from it and now I'm slowly getting back into it. I've got my own special beliefs in the Lord. I'm one of those kind of people who doesn't force my religion on others. If you don't want to hear it, I don't say it. It's a personal thing, a friendship I have with the Lord.

'I talk to the Lord often, even before games. I ask Him to protect all the players. I ask Him to help me play to the best of my ability and for strength to always go the distance and never give up. I pray for other people, some who are ill or have problems. I pray for my family and for the future. I read my Bible because it is a good guide for life. Most importantly I am honest with the Lord. My heart is an open book before God. He knows what is inside anyway, but I let Him know what I'm feeling anyway.'

Lomu is happier praying silently sitting next to the small lake in his garden or spending an hour by the ocean or on some remote hill, gazing in wonderment at God's creation. 'My relationship with God is more than sitting in church or doing the right things. I would rather spend time alone meditating on the word of God or just waiting on the Lord. It is so important to me to have the space and time to be on my own with the Lord.

'One of the reasons I wanted to live here is because I knew it would be a refuge from the other life I lead as an All Black and sports celebrity. But even so I still feel the need to get out in the country now and again. New Zealand is such a beautiful country, I wouldn't want to live anywhere else, except Tonga maybe, but only when I retire from rugby. Maybe then the time will be right to return to my roots for good.'

5 SEARCHING FOR THE TRUTH

The past can really f*** with you.

Mike Tyson

He just stood there looking for all the world like a character out of Lee Tamahori's *Once Were Warriors*. Black leather and chains and a facial tattoo. 'What the f*** are you staring at?' he shouted and ran across the road to confront me, his face taut with anger, lips snarling and eyes popping out of his head. 'Jesus, motherf***er, you'd better have a f***in' good reason,' and suddenly he was right in my face. I could see red veins in the eyes and scars between the perfect black tattoo patterns. The design was perfectly executed, a work of art. 'Nice job,' I said.

'Nice what? F***er,' he retorted, 'what's f***in' nice? White bitch.'

'Your tattoo,' I said, my heart racing as I prepared for what seemed like an inevitable violent confrontation with Billy, the half-Maori gang member who said he could help me find out the truth about the murder of Jonah Lomu's uncle and cousin. I needed Billy's help to nail down the

---

reality of Lomu's past but right now it looked as though I should have listened to the advice given to me at the Mangere Bridge Community police office. 'Don't hang around after dark in Mangere East,' they warned, 'and don't even get out of the car in Otara, unless you stay on the main street where the shopping centre is. It's not safe.'

Their words, and images of Tamahori's shockingly violent account of Maori life in South Auckland, came back to haunt me as I faced Billy on a deserted street on downtown Otara, close to where Lomu's uncle and cousin were hacked to death. I was here on a hunch that some other guy was telling the truth, but the truth doesn't seem that important when you're about to find out just how mean a crazed half-Maori can get. 'Are you Billy?' I asked, frantically, and backed away quickly because he had a look in his eyes that said attack first, ask questions later.

'F*** you,' he snarled and spat on my boots.

'Hey, cool it,' I shouted, 'just chill out one second.' My words came out fast and breathless because there wasn't time to think. 'I don't want to fight you. At least respect me for having the balls to meet you. Come on, come on, just chill for a moment.' I held out my hand, a desperate gesture of some kind of friendship in this moment of madness. Billy appeared to relax slightly. The tension in his face eased, his clenched fists dropped to his sides. 'Don't f*** with me,' he said.

'I won't. I just want to talk. Let me talk. Let's chill out for a bit and talk. It's cool, really.' My hand remained outstretched. He looked at it and looked in my eyes and looked around to see if anyone he knew was watching what he was about to do.

'Okay, bro,' he said softly and reached out his hand. He touched my hand, not shaking it, but closing his hand around mine so that it made a soft fist. Not a fist of anger but a fist of respect. He tapped his knuckles against mine. 'Chilled. Definitely chilled.'

Billy wanted money, 100 dollars, for a couple of hours of his time. Time to tell me everything he knew about Lomu and what had happened to Lomu's uncle and cousin. It was a small price to pay for inside information; street secrets, some of which had already been revealed to me to make a mockery of all the media hype about Lomu's so-called troubled past on South Auckland's violent streets.

'Can I trust you?' I asked Billy. The question was not as stupid as it sounds because in three days on the streets and in homes of Mangere and Otara I had learned one valuable lesson. If you're honest and straight with a Polynesian, they won't turn you over. It's an unwritten law in the code of their culture. Sure, Billy was a bit rough around the edges with a bad attitude and a criminal record to match, but there was sincerity in his eyes and voice when he said: 'Yeah, as long as you don't f*** with me. If you do I'll kill you, but if you don't I'll treat you like a bro.'

In the end Billy was true to his word, but before his story can unfold any further, we have to turn the clock back 24 hours to Friday 28 August 1998. That was the day I began to discover the truth about Jonah Lomu's past and eventually set up a meeting with Billy, but not before I met Pau and Mellie and Lomu's mother and father, Hepi and Semisi, and a tough young Tongan called Bull. Most of the drama unfolded right outside the Lomu family home at Maitland Place, a quiet cul-de-sac in the heart of East Mangere, where I discovered that many of the things said about Jonah Lomu in the media, especially the British press, are a distortion of reality, and in

Otara where, during a potentially dangerous meeting in a former Maori gang hideout, more missing pieces of Lomu's young life fell into place.

At the age of 24 Jonah Lomu hasn't experienced enough of life or accomplished enough to justify the premature and over-hyped image of a legend born out of trouble and strife; some kind of good-from-bad ghetto hero. Lomu is no Mike Tyson. He was bad and is bad and really did punch, kick and stab his way out of the ghetto. When it comes to troubled childhoods, Lomu is not in Tyson's league. In fact Jonah had it easy because he had a strong, caring and strict family to keep him on the right path. The bottom line, which may embarrass the sensationalists, is that Jonah Lomu is basically a nice, shy boy who hasn't got a malicious bone in his body and would prob-ably have settled for a career as a bank officer in South Auckland had rugby not catapulted him to mega-stardom.

The problem has been – and it's a common one – that rumours and hype have distorted the truth. Young fans have started to believe that rugby really did save Jonah Lomu from a life of crime and possibly early death. It sounds better, sells a product that fits the image of a *Once Were Warriors*-type hero, battle-scarred and haunted by a violent past and yet striving against the odds to become someone. Tyson is a money-making machine, a promoter's dream, despite his psycho-pathic tendencies, but what if he really changed from sinner to saint, then what? Would he still captivate the morbid interest of the sporting world? Would people be as desperate to watch him? Would he give them the same kick? Definitely not, and so Lomu's cranked-up past has been allowed to get away from the less sensational truth and the marketing men are happy. A soft, shy and sometimes scared 24-year-old who misses his mother and looks up to his father and adores his wife is less likely to appeal to the masses than a ghetto-toughened hardman who fears no one and has the scars to prove it.

Lomu does have scars on his arms and body, a testimony to the time he was involved in fights with other boys during his schooldays in Mangere. His uncle was decapitated, his body chopped into pieces in a machete attack, and his cousin died after being stabbed in the chest, his wrists slit and stomach cut out. Lomu saw their bodies, or what was left of them. He was a young boy, approaching his thirteenth birthday, and the memory stayed with him for a long time. But there is more good in his past than bad, more peace than violence, more normality than abnormality. In fact the only thing that really stands out during his growing up in South Auckland is Lomu's unique sporting talent. He is a natural athlete and was head and shoulders above his peers, literally. Jonah stood out from the crowd – he was well over six feet by the time he started senior school – and it's the main reason why he became involved in the skirmishes between rival gangs at school, why other less scrupulous youths tried to get him into trouble. The truth is that Hepi Lomu was never going to let her boy veer off the straight and narrow. She is a strong-willed, high-principled, religious woman who was not afraid to pack Jonah off to a strict Methodist-based boarding school to make sure he had the opportunity to fulfil the great potential in his genetically superior body.

On the day I first met Hepi and her husband Semisi, a lay preacher who plays a highly active and influential role in the local church, I discovered another truth about Jonah, the only parallel to Tyson's rags-to-riches story. Despite being born with a will to survive and succeed in the face of overwhelming odds, Lomu, like Tyson, was bullied as a child. He was bigger and stronger than all the other kids but he was not confident in his own ability to be his own person, or comfortable with who he was. He became a victim, something of a freak of nature; a giant boy with a gentle spirit who desperately wanted to fit in but didn't know how. In the end it was easier to go with the flow and Jonah might easily have ended up on the wrong side of the law. That's why Hepi sent him to boarding school, among other reasons, including a desire for her son to be educated, nurtured and influenced by Methodists. Lomu's ancestors were taught by Methodist missionaries who arrived in Tonga armed with the Bible and the promise of a better life born out of education and faith in God. Hepi and Semisi both agreed that sending their son to the disciplinarian Wesley College, south of Manukau, was in Jonah's very best interests. They were right.

Two hours before I ended up drinking tea and eating biscuits as a guest of Hepi and Semisi Lomu's next door neighbours Pau and Mellie, I bumped into Bull, a couple of blocks away from Maitland Place. He was walking down the road and I was lost. It's easy to get lost in Mangere. Most of the streets look the same, basic wooden houses behind wire mesh fencing, miles and miles of downtrodden Polynesian suburbia, but the streets aren't as mean as some make out. I arrived at Mangere Bridge, a pretty, bustling community populated mainly by white New Zealanders, half an hour's drive from the city on the other side of the Mangere Bridge that crosses the Manukau Harbour, which feeds the various creeks that irrigate the north-west of Manukau.

Mangere Bridge is an outpost, the last call before it gets rough, or so they told me. In truth, with the exception of one particular place in downtown Otara, there is not one area of Manukau that is tourist-unfriendly. Obviously there are areas of every major city that are best avoided after dark, but Mangere is not one of them, despite the claims of two certain ladies, who we'll call Betsy and Rose because they asked for anonymity, and a police officer who acted with such anti-Polynesian hostility he could have been the white cop out of Spike Lee's *Do The Right Thing* – the one who loved to hate every colour but his own.

It was a beautiful afternoon. The sun was out and the sky as blue as the ocean; it was hard to believe it was winter. The temperature was up in the late sixties and, after several days of heavy rain and fog, people were walking around in shorts and T-shirts, and less, as I drove down the main shopping street before parking the rented hatchback in a space in front of a food store. I knew Jonah's parents still lived in Mangere, but it's a big place and I hadn't a clue where to start. So I headed down the street looking for someone to ask and that's when I saw the Mangere Community Police sign above the door of a small office set back from the main road. I walked over, the door was wide open, and I stepped inside. No police officers, only two strangely dressed ladies in their sixties, maybe older. Betsy, who must weigh more than Lomu but had kindness glowing on her face in a warm, attractive kind of way, sat behind the counter. Rose, older and a hundred times thinner, stood a few feet away. She looked like a cross between the cartoon lady owner of Tweety-Pie and Woody Allen, only behind a ridiculously large pink pair of heavily glazed horn-rimmed glasses, Rose's eyes were magnified and distorted so that they looked like shiny golf balls, rolling around as though attached to springs. Rose had eyes like you find on the end of joke shop glasses.

'Can we help you?' Betsy and Rose said in unison. I couldn't take my eyes off Rose's eyes until Betsy stood up and for the first time in my life I saw what appeared to be a seven-foot woman. Not only was she heavier than Jonah, she had him beat vertically by a good few inches. Rose was dwarfed, like Tweety-Pie standing next to Big Bird. And then I noticed Rose only had one set of teeth. Her bottom gum was as bare as the flesh under her wig because her dentures were proving uncomfortable. Both wore garish floral dresses that must have been designed during the 50s and more strings of fake pearls than the cheap jewellery stall at Stoke market. 'Can we help you?' they asked again in perfectly synchronized, wavery voices.

'I'm not sure,' I answered. 'I'm trying to find where Jonah Lomu's parents live. I'm a writer from England. I'm researching a book.'

Betsy looked down at Rose and Rose looked at me. 'The Lomus,' Betsy said. 'Well I'm not sure, but I think they are in Mangere East. Rose, pass me the phone book.'

'I've already looked,' I said, 'they aren't in it.' There are actually two Lomus in the Auckland phone book, one in a place I've never heard of and one in Mangere. I called them both on the phone from my hotel room in the city only to find they were not related to Jonah Lomu, or so they claimed.

'Well,' said Betsy, 'the only thing I can suggest is that you drive into Mangere East and ask someone. I'm pretty sure Jonah's parents still live there, in fact I'm certain of it. What do you think Rose?'

Rose thought for a moment and removed her glasses to clean one of the lenses with a tissue. At last her eyes were normal. It was just her glasses. Kaleidoscope glasses. 'Do you think he'll be all right going to Mangere East?' Rose answered, but the phone had just rung and Betsy was busy quizzing some troubled Mangere Bridge resident about a vandalized fence.

'You should be okay down there,' Rose continued. 'Just don't get out of your car.'

'Why?' I asked.

'Well it's a bit rough in Mangere East. There is a lot of crime there because of the gangs. There is a lot of unemployment and you could get robbed or worse. But in the daylight you should be all right.'

'Well, I'll come back and haunt you if you're wrong,' I joked.

'Oh no, I'm not taking responsibility,' she said, seriously before putting her big pink glasses back on. Her eyes looked like shiny golf balls again, so I left.

In the mid-80s things were pretty rough in the poor Polynesian areas of Mangere East. Impoverished housing estates sandwiched in between the international airport and the more comfortable suburbs of Otahuhu often boiled over with the frustration of unemployment and inter-racial disharmony. Today things are different in the district where Jonah Lomu grew up. It was never as bad as places like the Brooklyn ghettos where Tyson grew up, or even some places in the United Kingdom. I met a Scotsman in Otara who has worked in New Zealand for 12 years. He grew up in the poorest area of Glasgow before escaping to university where he studied electrical engineering, to become a specialist in the installation of high-tech fuel measuring equipment used by airlines. 'It's a myth that Mangere and Otara are vicious areas,' he told me. 'I first came here in 1986 and spend on average three months a year in Otara. I live with friends instead of in hotels, mainly because Otara is closer to the airport than the city. When people talk about mean streets and tough neighbourhoods, places like Glasgow, Liverpool and Manchester spring to mind. I've spent time in the Bronx in New York and in townships in Johannesburg and they are places where your life could be in danger if you end up in the wrong place at the wrong time. But South Auckland is a picnic. Even the so-called mean streets of Otara are less trouble than downtown Glasgow on a Saturday night. It's a myth, a load of rubbish.'

I remembered his words and Rose's warning as I headed down the long and winding Massey Road into Mangere East. I pulled into a petrol station for fuel and it was there I met the police officer, who advised me not to trust anyone in Mangere East unless they were either wearing a police uniform or white – or ideally both. 'Jonah Lomu, eh,' he said with a touch of sarcasm in his voice. 'Great player.'

'You don't rate him?' I asked.

'He's okay, when he's fully fit, which isn't often, but he's definitely not worth putting yourself at risk for, although I guess it's all in a day's work for you, eh?'

I said 'Not exactly.' He told me a couple of horror stories about robbery and assault, how Pacific Islanders and New Zealand Maori can't be trusted and why they hate white people – 'because they just do' – and then he got in his squad car and shouted, 'Good luck, you'll need it.'

Massey Road seemed to go on for ever but the longer it did the more I liked what I saw. Mangere is beautiful, in a simple kind of way, pretty churches and houses, clean and green, with a backdrop of lush hills and evergreen tress. Even when you get towards Mangere town centre, a few miles out of Mangere Bridge, where there is less money and higher unemployment and kids run around barefoot amid broken chairs, scrap domestic appliances and rusty, jacked-up cars and pick-ups, there is still a good feel about the place.

I stopped at another petrol station where the assistant, a Tongan woman in her forties, told me that Hepi and Semisi Lomu called in most days for fuel and other supplies, although she wasn't sure exactly where they lived. So I headed out again, turning off Massey Road by the side of a huge Samoan church, hoping for a slice of luck and praying for safety, even though I couldn't believe all the hype about these so-called mean streets. It was then I saw Bull. A big, mean-looking Tongan guy in his late teens or early twenties wearing a leather jacket with the word 'Bloods' painted in red on the back. No facial tattoo but a nasty-looking scar in the shape of a crescent moon – wider in the middle – from his ear to the corner of his mouth.

It was too late to turn back now. Because it would be dark in a few hours and I was so close to tracking down Lomu's parents I stopped the car, got out and shouted: 'Excuse me, do you speak English?'

Bull stopped and looked in my direction. He was built like a bull, a Tongan Tyson I thought, but to my surprise he smiled and said: 'Sure man, what do you want?'

I walked over and introduced myself, telling him what I was doing in Mangere East and why it was so important to get in touch with Jonah Lomu's parents. Bull laughed and slapped me on the back. 'It's your lucky day, man,' he said and walked over to my car and got in. 'Come on,' he shouted, 'I want you to meet my sister.'

We drove two or three blocks to the house where Bull lives with his sister Grace and her husband Lee. Bull never said another word until he fetched Grace out of the house to meet me. 'Look man, Grace will take you to where Jonah's folks live, but you must come back later to see me. If you are writing a book about him you should meet this guy I know. He knows all about Jonah's past. He knew Jonah's uncle, you know the one who was killed in Otara.'

I couldn't believe my good fortune and told Bull I'd return later. I did and he set up a meeting with Billy, the tattoo-faced Maori. Grace directed me down two or three streets before pointing to a sign that said 'Maitland Place'. 'They live at the house at the top, number 8a,' she said.

'I can't thank you enough,' I told her. 'You know I was warned not to come here. They told me not to get out of the car. They gave the impression that Mangere East is a bad place, but everyone I have met today has been so genuine and kind. I like it here.'

Grace smiled. 'We don't bite,' she laughed, softly. 'We're not gonna eat you,' and she laughed louder. 'Most of the people who make up stories about this place have never even been here. The newspapers make up stories about Jonah Lomu growing up in such a terrible place but they have never bothered to find out if it's true. I'm glad you came. Go tell the world what we are really like.'

'Yes I will,' I told Grace and drove her home. 'Tell Bull I'll call later. Maybe I can buy him a drink.'

She shook my hand and said something in Tongan I didn't understand. 'I've just asked God to bless you,' she said.

'I think He already has.'

Hepi and Semisi were not at home. The humble green and white wooden one-storey house was empty. The only sign of life was a mean-looking old black dog who I later found out from Pau had no teeth. The house is surrounded by a wire mesh fence on two sides and a pink corrugated fence divides it from Pau and Mellie's property. There is a small white wooden letterbox on a post with '8a' on the front and a garage at the top of the drive that has seen better days. The front garden is tidy with a small tree and a couple of bushes but the back yard is untidy, like a scrap heap, with discarded furniture and piles of wood and bags of vegetables stacked on makeshift tables.

There is one of those rotary washing lines in the middle of the back yard and the following day, when I visited Maitland Place for the second time, Semisi hung things on it that you wouldn't see in a million years in England, or most other places for that matter. The old leather-skinned Tongan lay preacher, who wasn't at home the previous afternoon when I first met his wife Hepi, pulled up in a used black 3 series BMW with wide wheels, got out, opened the boot and hauled out four dead pigs. Each one had been clubbed to death, a Tongan custom, and Semisi strung each one out on that rotary washing line just as he might have been hanging out wet clothes.

They hung there, heads down, while Jonah Lomu's father prepared a fire in a pit in the back yard. He was going to cook the pigs to eat at church the following day. Sunday is devoted entirely to church and the people share a meal. Smoked pig is the main course. Jonah Lomu has seen his father do this many times and when he was living at Maitland Place before the All Blacks changed his life the young Lomu only wanted to be like Semisi; a strong family man with faith in God.

Sunday is the most important day of the week for Polynesians. The church comes before anything else, even the well-being of the children. Pacific Islanders living in the poorest part of South Auckland, Mangere East and downtown Otara, often complain that their schools, nurseries, libraries, community centres and health centres are underfunded. They want more money from the government. But the churches never go short, in fact they are very rich. When Jonah Lomu was growing up in Mangere East he saw a lot of his parents' income going to the church while he was being denied things like new shoes or trainers or clothes. A Tongan taxi driver told me: 'You will see kids around here who have little in the way of material comfort, but go and look at the churches. That is where a big percentage of the average Tongan wage goes. The church prospers, the people don't. It's a controversial subject. Polynesians say, "We need more money for health and education," and the Pakeha reply, "Stop giving so much away to the church then." '

But it's the Tongan way and the way of other Island groups like the Samoans and Fijians. Tongans have a vigorous work ethic, the man leaving the house during the day and taking any work as it comes along and the woman on any shift work available, often cleaning jobs. With tithes to the church and money sent to the extended family back home, there is not much left after the rent has been paid.

Both Jonah Lomu's parents still work even though he is a multi-millionaire. Semisi and Hepi are in their forties and will probably work until they are 60, such is the Tongan way. Allegedly, they have more than $1 million tucked away in bank accounts as a result of Jonah's success during the past few years but there is no evidence of any wealth at Maitland Place. They choose to continue their humble lives. They don't want it any other way.

The day before I watched Semisi stringing the dead pigs out on the washing line, I spent several hours next door, at 8

Maitland Place, as a guest of Pau and Mellie, waiting for Hepi to come home from work. Pau is older than Jonah but he remembers the days when Lomu used to hang around outside his house with the other kids, throwing an old rugby ball around. 'It seems like yesterday,' Pau said as he sat on a sofa with a nylon-strung guitar in his arms. Most Tongans can hold a tune. I couldn't believe just how good Pau was. He plays and sings well but so do Semisi and Hepi and Jonah. Semisi loves the keyboard and Hepi has a good voice. Jonah has a sweet voice for such a big guy and is thinking about taking up an instrument, probably the guitar.

'Jonah is an intelligent, sensitive kind of guy,' Pau continued. 'He was a good kid, always wanting to help people. He wasn't always an angel but he never did anything really bad. All the stories about him running with gangs and living a life of petty crime are not true. Hepi is a strong influence in his life. She made sure Jonah stayed on the right path. It's thanks to her that he is where he is today.'

Jonah may have been more protected by his parents, especially his mother, than other children of his age, but there is some evidence that he was not entirely immune to the rougher expressions of social deprivation and frustration. Later, when he reflected on his childhood, he would compare the tough world of Mangere East with Tonga, the land of his forefathers. While in the first 'one had to live by one's wits and instincts, some of the time ... and bad things did happen', in Tonga Jonah drew comfort from nature and the essential underlying sense of a peaceful, honest community.

Two of the bad things that did happen were in 1986. A group of Jonah's male friends surrounded and threatened to sexually assault a teenage girl. The incident disturbed Lomu because he wanted no part of such behaviour. When the same male friends robbed and beat up a young Samoan boy, Jonah tried to stop them but ended up getting kicked in the face and ribs. He was lucky to escape serious injury.

Running the daily gauntlet of going to school toughened Lomu up. He was basically an easy-going, unassuming boy, but he possessed an unbreakable, free spirit. Like his father, Jonah has a brave heart and pride that has roots deep in Tongan culture. His ancestors were among the most courageous of the Pacific Island people. They would rather die than lose dignity, and yet Tongans are slow to anger. It takes a lot of abuse to provoke Tongan wrath. Jonah would more often walk away from trouble than face it head on, although there were times when he stood his ground and then someone, mainly the other guy or guys, got badly hurt.

'I could look after myself,' he recalled. 'You either fought your way home from school or arrived back with a black eye and without clothes or bag. The bullies used to go out what we call "stocking". They'd have a shopping list and if they saw you wearing anything that was on it, they'd just take it. Sometimes it wasn't worth getting beat up for but other times I stood my ground. If you said no to anyone it was because you could look after yourself. I didn't take any crap. My parents taught me about strength of mind and self-belief. My father is a strong man physically but also mentally. Strength of mind is more important than physical strength.'

Jonah looks more like his mother, but inside there is a mirror image of his father. Strong and silent, humble but proud, God-fearing but afraid of no man. Semisi came from respected Tongan stock and was brought up, like his future wife, in a cramped wooden home, torn down and rebuilt several times because of hurricane damage. It was a poor community of fishermen and farmers, struggling with hardship. Semisi, a distinguished-looking man, not as big as his son but nevertheless powerful, taught Jonah to defend himself but never encouraged violence. Semisi, so the story goes, had a reputation as a bit of a tough guy as a young man growing up in Tonga, but his strong moral values kept his wild side in check.

There is a bit of this macho hot-headedness in Jonah. During his early teens he almost went off the rails and it took a firm hand from Semisi and Hepi to keep him in line. 'It was a bad phase,' Jonah recalls. 'I wanted to be a tough guy. At one stage I got really close to going out of control. My temper was wild, which was not the way I was born. From a shy kind of boy who didn't have a malicious bone in his body, I became a seriously angry person. If I lost it back then, look out. Even if someone was just staring at me, it used to annoy me. I'd walk straight across to him. No questions. It was bang, right in the face. I was 12 years old and I had a bad attitude. It's the way it was back then in the mid-80s, everyone trying to be macho, trying to make a name for themselves.'

For Jonah life was black and white at that time, or more to the point black and blue and sometimes red as the blood flowed during violent clashes with the other wannabe tough guys. 'I think a lot of the kids from South Auckland were feeling the same things. Anger, frustration, wanting to be noticed, desperate to be someone who people looked up to or feared. What happened back then straightened out my life. I've been stabbed a few times and been kicked across my chest by steel-capped boots. It was all part of growing up because, if you didn't know how to fight, you weren't going to survive long.'

There are stories and there is truth. The truth is less shocking. Lomu admits that some of the rumours about his violent passage between childhood in poor and difficult Mangere and adulthood amid all the material rewards of his new-found wealth are completely false. Some of the things Lomu is supposed to have done are myths dreamed up by people who have never even visited Mangere or Otara, although he was exposed to, and participated in, acts of violence during an often dangerous existence in the volatile climate of South Auckland's Polynesian suburbs. There were times when Lomu sailed close to the wind and, as the truth about his past unravelled, it became clear that some of the missing pieces of his young life are jagged with real danger. However, when I showed Pau and Bull a list of Lomu-related incidents, taken from the pages of newspapers and magazines, recalled from memories of hearsay during my career as a sports writer: Jonah is shot three times during a gang fight but still finds the strength to almost kill the gunman with a baseball bat; Jonah steals a car and burns it, leaving the blazing wreckage somewhere down Massey Road; Jonah stabs a rival gang member in the chest and leaves him close to death, escaping conviction through intimidation of the victim's family; Jonah runs drugs out of Mangere and starts a turf war that results in the murder of his uncle and cousin – they almost fell over laughing when they read these fictitious accounts of Lomu's past. All lies, complete fabrication.

'I doubt anyone would have bothered to make these stories up had Jonah not become famous,' said Bull, who is the same age as Lomu and remembers him walking past his parents' house to school. 'I think he had a couple of fights where the other guy pulled out a knife and cut his arm,' Bull continued.

'I remember him getting beat up pretty badly one summer. He got jumped by a few guys and they gave him a good kicking. I think Jonah's problem was that he was a good-looking kid who was head and shoulders above everyone else, in terms of size and strength and ability as an athlete. Other kids were jealous and Jonah became a target. Back then it was pretty rough at times, but nothing like the horror stories people have been making up.'

Bull was telling the truth. It was good enough for me, but I wanted to hear it from Hepi and Semisi and I wanted to meet Billy, the Maori gang member who knew something about the tragic death of Jonah's uncle and cousin in Otara, because it was their shocking murder that changed Lomu's life.

6 THE NATURAL

**She knows there's no success like
failure, and that failure's no success
at all.**

Bob Dylan

Hepi Lomu was insistent that Jonah should leave Mangere and go to Wesley College, although her mind was made up before the Otara killings. That incident was the ultimate catalyst in bringing to an end Jonah Lomu's existence as an angry young man on the streets on South Auckland's poorest areas, from Mangere East to Otara, Papatoetoe to Mt. Richmond and the city limits – 16 square miles of potential trouble. Hepi began to hear things that troubled her, stories about Jonah beginning to make a name for himself as some kind of up-and-coming rebel on the block, and it was worse than just the unpredictable and often volatile moods of adolescence.

Sure, the young Lomu was searching for self-identity and independence, he was changing from a child into a young adult and the fire of passion that raged inside him was as natural and necessary as his mother's instinct to nurture and protect, but something else was happening, another powerful force was at work, and it was this that worried Hepi. There was something dark rising from the streets of Otara, a brooding whisper of bad intent. Before long it might lure Jonah to places where bad things happen, desperate corners of broken society and poisoned humanity where hate and violence and greed breed death. Hepi knew she couldn't afford to take any chances with the future of her son, especially after what the dark power had done to the Lomu family. 'Force the hand of fate,' she thought, 'choose life for Jonah, choose it now.'

Billy was my only chance to uncover the real truth; that became as clear as the waters of the Waikato after Hepi and Semisi refused to dig up the past. Maybe it was too painful, maybe they didn't want me to find out that Jonah had been in deeper than they said he was, but for whatever reason I ended up leaving Maitland Place for the last time with little else but the bare facts of the Otara incident rattling around in my mind like old bones. The story is shocking enough without slicing open the scars of deep wounds but if there is a skeleton I had to at least try to re-animate flesh and blood. Billy, I was sure, could help me find the missing pieces of a human jigsaw.

Ironically, it was a tattoo, or at least the desire to have one, that could have thwarted Hepi Lomu's plan to radically alter the course and content of Jonah's life, and it was outside a tattoo parlour in Otara that I finally realized just how close Jonah Lomu came to the point of no return. By all accounts this was the critical moment of a short span of time, probably less than 12 months, when Lomu's life could have easily gone off the rails. Easily because there were moments when even

Hepi Lomu had no control over her headstrong son. Exactly how close Jonah came to throwing away his natural born talent remains unclear – only he knows the facts of what took place in the months leading up to his first teenage year – but what is certain is that, for a moment long enough to create real danger, he lost his way in life and had to make a decision to find it again, or reap the consequences. His father Semisi painted a different picture of Jonah from the one Billy would eventually create, but Lomu senior, or Hepi, are not prepared to reveal family secrets that will probably accompany them and Jonah to the grave. Maybe in time it will all come out, and perhaps it won't be worth the wait because of the likely unimportance of it all, but for now we have only Jonah's admission that he came close to wasting his life, his parents' somewhat clouded insight into the past, and the partially substantiated claims of three men who share a slice of Lomu's life before rugby.

Semisi did little to settle the situation. He was leaning on the fence between his and Pau and Mellie's home with the washing line of dead pigs as a surreal backdrop. 'I haven't got all the answers for you,' he said. 'Only Jonah knows what happened.' Semisi wasn't comfortable with the line of questioning. Pau and Bull had already laughed off a whole list of rumours about Jonah's past but I asked Semisi to confirm or deny something that I had heard from a former school mate of Jonah.

The man in question, who asked to remain anonymous because he lives only two blocks from Maitland Place, told me that, at the age of 13, Lomu had a price on his head. 'For several months Jonah had been throwing his weight around, getting more aggressive, more cocky, and he would not think twice about using violence to stamp his mark on the neighbourhood.

He looked older than he was and the word got around that there was this arrogant Islander kid with a reputation for fighting all the time who wasn't afraid of anyone and was bad-mouthing people. It was getting out of control, I don't think Jonah knew just how bad, but a lot of people who were around at that time believe that had he not been sent to college, he would have ended up like his uncle and cousin.'

I pressed Semisi for an answer, reminding him that Jonah had already admitted to acts of premeditated violence during his adolescence. 'He got into a few fights but nothing more serious than that,' came the reply. I noticed that Semisi had become agitated. He stood back from the fence and frowned. 'Look,' he said, raising his voice. 'Jonah went through a difficult time, it was difficult for this family. He got involved with some bad people who would have hurt him had he not left the area. But none of this matters now, so leave it.' I had no choice so I went to Otara to meet Billy, who told me a story that chilled me to the bone.

The drive from Mangere East to Otara is less than six miles but it felt like forever as I prepared to face Billy again, even though I had his word that 'as long as I didn't f*** with him' everything would be cool. The sun was out and Otara looked inviting in a strange way. Weber Brothers' circus was in town and kids were crowding outside the big tent and playing in the park next door, shooting basketball and riding the swings and roundabouts. But my directions, scrawled in black pen on the back of a hastily torn piece of dirty card, were for out of town, down to gangland on the East Tamaki Road where I'd arranged to meet Billy outside a tattoo parlour called Polynesian Tattoo. 'You can't miss it,' he said. 'There's a picture of a snake coiled around a palm tree on the side of the building. Don't go in though, we'll talk somewhere else.'

I found the place and drove past. The snake and the palm tree and the Polynesian Tattoo sign were clearly visible, and there were two Harley Davidsons parked outside, but Billy was nowhere to be seen. I was a few minutes early so I turned into a Super Liquor store and bought a case of Lion Red beer. Billy wanted booze and cash for his time. It was a judgement call but after all the good that came out of my time in Mangere I believed Billy would also come through, and he did.

'Didn't expect to see you again,' he said and got into the car. I asked why and he laughed. 'Glad to see you got the booze. Got a few bucks as well?' I pulled out a few notes, five $10 bills, and handed them over.

'It's all I've got on me,' I said, half expecting Billy to turn his nose up, but he didn't. Instead he counted the money and stuffed it down the side of his leather motorbike boots. 'Okay bro, let's go,' he said, nodding in the direction of the Super Liquor store. 'Keep driving and I'll tell you where to go.' We drove for ten, maybe fifteen minutes before Billy spotted the place where he wanted to talk, an old wooden and corrugated iron warehouse at the end of a deserted stretch of road. Not far away, Otara Creek flowed lazily by before widening out into Curlew Bay. From here you can take a boat out into the deeper waters of Hauraki Gulf, sail around the north tip of the Coromandel Peninsula, past its rugged mountains, subtropical forests, volcanic hills, and white-sand bays; through the Colville Channel and beneath Great Barrier Island and into the vastness of the Pacific Ocean. 'I was born close to here,' Billy said. 'In the back seat of a wrecked car. That's what my mother told me. She's dead now. Overdosed on some bad shit.'

'What about your father?' I asked, noticing that Billy had tattoos on his arms and hands as well as his face.

'Never knew him, probably some drunken bastard who f***ed my mother and then pissed off.' Billy reached behind and pulled a can of Lion Red from the case. 'Want one?' he asked. 'Sure,' I said and we sat looking out over Otara Creek, drinking beer and talking about his past, my past and our hopes and fears and of course Jonah Lomu, the reason we were here at all. Billy is the same age as Jonah, although he looks older, probably because life has not been kind to him. He was born not far from Maitland Place in Mangere East. His mother and two sisters, one of whom is also dead – killed by a drunken boyfriend – and the other who lives somewhere in America but never stayed in touch, moved with Billy to a sea village in the Bay of Plenty, only to end up sharing a house with prostitutes and drug dealers in the most deprived part of Otara. 'Maketu is beautiful,' he said, thinking about the sun-warmed town on the shore of the Bay of Plenty, 'and one day I will go back and live there until I die. If I stay here I won't live as long,' and the lines on his face appeared to darken as he thought about his existence in Otara.

From the age of seven to around nine or ten, Billy – short for William te Whaki Kahaturi – grew up in the same neighbourhood as Lomu and he remembers seeing him walking to school, getting involved in fights, and being exceptionally strong and quick. 'He was faster and stronger than anyone else his own age and older kids as well,' Billy said. 'But years later, when we came to Otara, I could not believe the stories I was hearing about Lomu. The kids in the gangs, especially the Black Power mob and the Black Dogs who controlled the streets where I grew up, kept going on about this kid in Mangere who was making a name for himself as some kind of tough guy. He was the nephew of a local tough guy who was into some bad stuff in Otara. That's how it all started.'

The run-down warehouse in front of us used to be a meeting place for Maori gang members and before that a storage facility for truck parts. Now it is empty. Billy and I went inside and sat on a steel lintel next to a hole in the roof space, where we drank more beer and looked down on Otara Creek. It was on the concrete floor beneath us that Billy suffered a broken jaw, fractured arm, and badly bruised ribs and face during his initiation; the moment he became a full-blooded gang member. He also had some of his tattoo work done here, but not the work of art on his face. That painful procedure was carried out in the home of a relative in Rotorua, around 35 miles from Maketu.

The city of Rotorua was settled by descendants of voyagers from the legendary Maori homeland of Hawaiki, thought to be the Tahitian island group, and still has the greatest concentration of Maori residents of any New Zealand centre. The entire region is situated on a volcanic rift which stretches in a 124-mile (200 km) line from White Island off the coast of the Bay of Plenty to Lake Taupo and the volcanoes of the Tongariro National Park in the Central Plateau of the North Island. Rotorua offers heaven and hell within walking distance of each other; a barren wasteland of rotten-smelling sulphur, cratered with scalding cauldrons, bubbling mud pools and roaring geysers, within sight of calm, azure, trout-filled lakes, lush forests and fresh, green pastures. It is one of the two jewels of New Zealand tourism – along with Queensland in the South Island – and a hot spot of Maori culture.

It took an elderly Maori man the best part of a day to complete Billy's facial tattoo. The son of the same tattoo artist moved to Mangere and worked out of Otara for several years; he is the man who was, allegedly, going to tattoo Lomu's arms and legs and face. 'I heard that Jonah wanted it done to make him even tougher in the eyes of his friends. He wanted to be a leader, someone people feared,' Billy said, 'but the reason it did not happen is because the tattoo artist found out that he was lying about his age. He said he was older when in fact he was only 13. Then he was sent away to Wesley and straightened out his life. Maybe it's good for him that he didn't end up like me.'

New Zealand Maori, who make up 15 per cent of the population, and other Pacific Islanders, the next largest group at six per cent – the result of large-scale immigration movements that began in the 1970s – are more tattooed than people anywhere else I have visited. The proliferation and mixing of the usual tribal European tattoos, serpents, bike insignia and naked ladies, and neo-traditional Maori *moko* – the famous curvilinear facial tattoos like those Billy has – is arresting to say the least. The most remarkable form of contemporary tattooing in New Zealand, however, is *Aotearoa*, the faithful adaptation of traditional Samoan techniques. Although censured by European Christian missionaries and not widely practised during the mid-century, Aotearoa was never abandoned altogether, and now flourishes both in Samoa and among Samoan migrants in New Zealand, especially in Mangere and Otara.

Although women bore punctures around their legs, Samoan tattooing was essentially an art form applied to male bodies. Bull, the Mangere resident who set up the meeting with Billy, is a case in point. His tattooed torso and legs would shock most people. The *pe'a*, as it is traditionally known, consists of a dense body of arched designs around the thighs, buttocks and lower back, applied with a comb-like tool that is dipped in pigment and then hammered repeatedly across the skin. The process is drawn-out and painful, and its accomplishment is essentially a rite of initiation, expressing deference to elders, as well as the maturity, knowledge and empowerment of the youth. Tattoos were formerly significant elements of the psychological armour of Samoan fighters. What they mark now is ethnic pride, which is not merely signified but compellingly demonstrated through this commitment of the body to a traditional art.

Only in New Zealand will you find guys like Bull and Billy, but I guess they are natural products of the cross-cultural stimulation that took place in the last century. Equally, the tattoo culture in the UK and Europe has its roots in Oceanic history because tattooing, originally a mainly Polynesian and Japanese tradition, has fascinated outsiders since its Oceanic manifestations were initially recognized by Europeans, by Cook's and Bligh's crews, in the late eighteenth century. The Enlightenment voyages of the British and the French marked the beginnings of imperialism in the region, but also inaugurated a fertile process of cross-cultural exchange. The emulation of Tahitian *tatau* by sailors and mutineers led to the widespread, eventually global, phenomenon of tattooing, while Tahitians adopted European motifs and imitated naval costumes in their own arts of the body.

Billy's bloodline goes right back to the days before these cultures collided and he taught me more about the history of the moko than I could have ever learned from books. On my return to England I checked out everything he told me and it was spot on, even the horror stories about the dark trade in tattooed skin. Tattoos are at once items in a natural history register and indefinably fascinating curiosities. Their bearers are often presented not as people, but as human types, and tattooed buttocks, legs, chests and even lips are frequently literally disembodied in both sketches and published engravings of the eighteenth and nineteenth centuries. This tendency reached its most extraordinary and shocking extreme in the collection of Maori men's moko in the form of preserved heads. When a member of Billy's gang died from a drug overdose they cut off his head and removed the skin from his face to preserve the moko.

Modern western society fears body art for many reasons. First, it's in our tradition to fear that with which we are not familiar. We, as a society, aren't self-assured and confident enough not to fear what made warriors fearsome for hundreds of years. Also, we associate this type of totally visible expression with an underlying destructive alternative lifestyle. People fear the 'hate tribe' of modern primitives just as they automatically fear skinheads. It's easier to hate the implications of the unknown than to ask and find out that the hate tribe is a group of people who are so directly and deeply offended by the state of ruination and complete absence of common decency in today's society that they intrusively and painfully decorate themselves in protest, as a visual representation of what most people choose not to even talk about. For the Maori of New Zealand, to have this form of facial tattooing was to hold one's status as a warrior. One without was a *papatea*, a plainface, a nobody.

Billy's face is covered with spiral scrolls, circles and curved lines, the lines and curves following the direction of the natural lines and indentations in his face. The tattoo extends from the throat to the roots of the hair. His forehead consists of a series of bars radiating out from a V-shaped centre. The nose is the central ornament as the most prominent feature on the face, and has spirals at the bridge and nostrils and at the tip. From the nose to the chin are three lines passing around the corners of the mouth. On the upper lip is a pattern scrolled horizontally. His cheek, jaw and chin are decorated with spirals. One distinctive feature of moko is that no two designs are ever alike, but what makes moko so impressive and awe-inspiring is the balance and symmetry of design, the minute accuracy in the detail, and the way that the spirals and curved lines echo the curvilinear shape of the human body.

The function of the tattoo for the warrior was and still is, in the case of modern-day 'fighters', not only an expression of social status, but also a conspicuous and frightening warning to the enemy, possibly about what a man who could endure having his lips tattooed could endure in battle. And should the moko fail to inspire fear, then it served to guarantee fame after death. The untattooed and the slaves were discarded, but a head with an impressive moko would be cut off and preserved on a pole. In the wars of the mid-1800s, the process evolved of trading the preserved, decapitated heads to sailors for guns and supplies. The sailors who kept souvenirs like these heads were the same ones who adopted tattooing techniques and brought them to the western world. The heads were also bargaining pieces in post-war peace negotiations. It was an important tribute to have one's head embalmed after death. It was mostly the chiefs and great warriors who were so honoured, and the heads were cured over a fire and kept as a memorial by the descendants.

The moko retained an important function in the afterlife. The Maori have a tradition that is actually common in many traditions all over the world. They believed that after death, elaborate facial tattoos would be consumed by a death hag who stood over the threshold of death. If she found tattoos to eat, she would pass her hand over the eyes of the person, imbuing them with the vision to find their way to the next world, but if they had no tattoos, she would eat their eyeballs, blinding the soul for all eternity. Similarly, the Newar of Bhaktapur, India, would use their tattoos as currency in heaven, just as the Ekoi of Nigeria would use scars. The Dyak depended on their tattoos to light the long dark passage to find their ancestors in the Apo-Kesio (the afterlife). And to the Sioux, tattoos were their passports to the land of the dead.

Among all of its functions, perhaps the most important purpose the moko serves is one of personal signature, or identity. Maoris believe that a moko imprints one's personality upon one's face. That's part of the reason that it was an act of reverence not only to keep the head of a deceased relative, but also to emulate his moko style. This endowed that member of the newer generation with traits like those honoured in his ancestor. This idea of the moko as representative of the entire identity is enhanced with consideration of its nature. It is such an ultimate accomplishment, signifying maturity, bravery and even sexuality, and is why so many feel that their tattoos are sort of a mask of their face tattooed onto the face.

Billy's face looked sad as the subject changed from Maori heritage to more recent memories of inter-racial tension in South Auckland. 'You know Jonah Lomu escaped because God gave him a natural talent, not because he hated life on the streets,' Billy said, sharply. 'I bet he's told you he's different, that he's not the same as me or Bull or any of the other guys who didn't make it. That's bullshit because Jonah Lomu is the same, he just got lucky. You can take someone out of the ghetto, but you can't always take the ghetto out of them. Ain't that the truth.'

I wasn't sure but late one night in a bar down on the Auckland waterfront, where you can hear the murky waters of Waitemata Harbour slap against the wooden wharves and see the Devonport lights shining across the bay, I met a group of New Zealand Tongans who said more or less the same thing. One of them was wearing a Jonah Lomu All Black top with the face of their hero splashed across the chest and the number 11 on the back. Three of the five guys had traditional tattoo designs on their arms and the two wearing cut-off jeans had tattoos on their legs also. One had half his face tattooed. We chatted about the state of New Zealand rugby and Lomu.

The brother-in-law of one of the guys was born in Mangere, only a stone's throw from Maitland Place. He is several years older than Jonah and left Mangere before Lomu's life started to get out of control. The brother of his wife said: 'There are lots of stories about Jonah's past. I don't know how much is true but from what I heard he was heading for big trouble. Rugby saved him, and I guess his mother played her part in getting him off the streets. But he loves the tough, aggressive image he's got, because he is tough and aggressive. He gets a kick out of kicking ass on the rugby field. He hasn't really changed since he was a wild teenager. My brother-in-law approached him outside a club once. He wanted his autograph for his son. He's a real decent guy, gentle as a lamb. But Lomu was in a foul mood and wouldn't sign. If my brother-in-law hadn't moved I reckon Lomu would have smacked him right in the face. But hey, he's only human and we love him really. He's a top guy and deserves all the success he can get, especially after the terrible illness that almost ruined his life. He's come up the tough way, so let's drink to Jonah. Lo ... muuu, Lo ... muuuu.' And their shouts drowned out the sound of the ocean.

Lomu tells a story about his past that virtually every newspaper in New Zealand and the UK has at some time or another printed as a favourite anecdote about the big man of rugby, although it may not be entirely accurate. He was 13 and sitting down somewhere on a street in Mangere, or it may have even been Otara, when a mugger came up and said, 'I want your shoes.' Lomu stood up, the mugger looked up, realized he was facing a boy-mountain and just said, 'Sorry, I've changed my mind,' and ran off.

'Yeah, I've heard that a few times,' Billy said ruefully, 'but I guess the truth wouldn't suit Jonah's image, you know, the poor kid from bad old Mangere who turned out to be a kind-hearted, charity-giving, filthy rich son of a bitch who makes the Pope look like Mad Max.'

'Why, didn't it happen like that?'

Billy smiled. 'Does it ever? Does it ever happen like they tell it after they start rubbing shoulders with the rich and famous? No, it didn't always happen like that. The real truth is Jonah used to love playing the victim. It was a game to him because he was born a freak, some kind of genetic accident. I mean, he was six and a half feet tall and 17 stone when he was 13. What's normal about that?'

So as Billy and I sat on the steel lintel next to the hole in the roof space and watched Otara Creek fade into the descending dusk he told me about the game Lomu used to play. How he would go looking for trouble, sit and wait for some street punk to find him. 'He knew he could handle himself, as long as the other guy didn't pull a blade or pop him with a pistol,' said Billy. 'But let me tell you, it would have happened sooner or later.'

I looked out of the hole in the roof and noticed how the setting sun set the water on fire. I imagined a blade or a bullet with Lomu's name on it and wondered how Hepi knew it was coming. 'Do you think Jonah's parents knew what he was getting into?' Billy scratched his head. 'Maybe,' he said, 'it's a pretty tight community in Mangere and Otara. There's always someone who knows someone who knows someone else. It's the grapevine kind of thing, but when the killing started, they knew for sure. It was a warning, fate maybe.'

Billy swung down off the lintel and landed on his feet. I did the same but staggered a little. 'Hey man, you need to get in shape,' he said, heading back to the road. 'Where are we going?' I shouted.

'Back into town. I'm gonna show you where it happened. We're going to the place where Jonah's uncle and cousin were killed. You'll like it, it's important to your book, and I always get a kick out of going there, anyway you may not believe what you are about to hear unless you see it with your own eyes.'

7 KILLER

When I lost my uncle I knew I was either going to end up like him or behind bars.

Jonah Lomu

ree Iupeliauro Iosefa Pauga. The words are green, encased in a black-outlined scroll and surrounded by red, yellow and blue flowers in a heart-shaped wreath. It is a beautifully designed and expertly executed tattoo, the work of a master craftsman. The woman wearing it, an attractive half-Maori girl in her early twenties, wanted the tattoo on her inner thigh but it would have been too painful, so she had it done on her back, just above her right shoulder blade. The tattoo is the size of an apple and if you look closely you can see the initials IIP in each of the flower heads. The girl pulled her jumper down at the back and turned around. She has brown eyes and the room lit up when she smiled. 'Fetch some beer for the guys, honey,' her husband said and smacked her buttocks as she walked past. 'Nice ass baby.' She turned her head and puckered her lips, teasing, revelling in her sexuality, before disappearing into the kitchen. 'Ain't she a doll,' he added, 'ain't she sex on legs. Back in a sec,' and he followed his wife into the kitchen.

I turned to face Billy. He was sitting in a chair, leaning back, puffing hard on a joint. 'Hey,' I said, 'Who is Iupeliauro Iosefa Pauga?'

Billy took another long puff on the joint, inhaling the smoke deep into his lungs and holding it there for 20 seconds or more. He breathed out, closed his eyes for a moment and laughed. 'Don't you know?' he answered.

'Obviously not. I wouldn't have asked otherwise.'

Billy stood up. 'Pauga is the man who killed Jonah Lomu's uncle,' he said before lowering his voice into a whisper and adding: 'Those two in the kitchen are his friends. They owe me a favour, so they will tell you anything you want to know, okay?'

I thought for a moment, looking around the untidy, cramped room. There were pictures of tattooed bodies on every wall and over in the corner an area set aside for tattooing. 'Who is he?' I asked, nodding in the direction of the kitchen. It was quiet in there. No voices, no chink of beer bottles, and a half-closed door. I was about to repeat my question when suddenly the door swung open and they came out with a crate of Export Gold and what smelled like a pot of meat stew. 'Okay boys, let's eat,' the husband said. 'Then we'll talk.'

His name is Sam and his wife's name is Stephanie. She is New Zealand Maori and he is of Tongan and Japanese ancestry, so he is half Tongan. Sam was born in Tokyo and is two years older than Jonah Lomu. His father is pure Tongan and is from the Islands, growing up in the same area as Semisi Lomu. Sam spent two years in Tonga, from the age of six to eight, and lived only a short distance from where Jonah spent six years of his life.

Since he was 13 Sam's life has revolved around Polynesian tattooing and this makes him unique, because most Tongans today are totally unaware of the fact that Tongans at one time were as heavily tattooed as most other Polynesians. He is one of only a handful of young Tongan men in nearly 200 years to wear the traditional Tongan tattoo. Remarkably he did the tattoo himself using traditional tools, tapping the design into his own skin and also teaching Stephanie to tattoo so that she could complete his backside. When Sam was a young teenager he wanted American and gang-style tattoos, like those a lot of the young Tongans and Samoans were wearing. Then one day he was looking through a book about Polynesia and saw a drawing of the Tongan man's tattoo. He knew he wanted to wear it and became more interested in the culture and started questioning his relatives. Most of them knew nothing about it, but then his grandmother told him that his grandfather, a friend of the parents of Semisi and Hepi Lomu, was one of the last men to wear the tattoo. Sam wanted that tattoo. It was like a part of his culture that was dead and he had a chance of reviving it.

The tradition of tattooing in Tonga was abandoned soon after European contact and the arrival of missionaries. At one time, nearly all Tongan males would have worn tattoos very similar to the *pe'a*, the traditional tattoo worn by Samoan men, like Bull. Women were tattooed as well in ancient Tonga, but the designs were limited to the arms and the inside of the hands and fingers. Tattooing was officially outlawed in 1838. Today, few Tongans even realize that their ancestors bore tattoos. Not only has the art been lost over the past two centuries, but the very knowledge of it is gone as well. According to Sam, who spent three years researching Tongan bloodlines, Jonah Lomu's fore-fathers were the last of the tattooed men on the island.

Tonga's story is interesting, and quite different from the other island groups in Polynesia, as Tonga has always remained independent. Tongans are exceptionally ingenious and very soon after European contact they styled their own monarchy after that of their visitors, retaining their own land and rule and readily adopting Christianity. They retained many aspects of their traditional culture, although other aspects have been lost entirely; lost even in the memories of the last elders. Knowledge of the old gods, the ancient religion and the tattoo are gone forever. Fortunately one of the early French explorers, Dumont d'Urville, included a detailed illustration of a Tongan man's tattoo in his journal. If it were not for this drawing we would know little about the appearance of the tattoo in Tonga.

The man's tattoo in Tonga was done in the same manner as the Samoan tattoo. The tool itself was a sharpened comb, made of either bone or shell. This was hafted onto a wooden handle. A second wooden tool served as a mallet, tapping the primary tool repeatedly, driving the comb into the skin. The pigment was soot collected from burning candlenut, a nut with a flammable oil. The soot was then mixed with either water or a fat until it reached the desired consistency. The process of tattooing in ancient Tonga was a long and painful one, particularly considering the amount of heavy black coverage in the tattoo. It was a mark of manhood and had fate gone the other way, Lomu could have ended up looking like Sam, although I was soon to find out the real reason why it never happened: it has more to do with the brutal killing that took place not far from where Sam and Stephanie live than Jonah's age.

When he was 17 Sam made tattoo tools based on the traditional Samoan tools he had seen. He used sewing needles attached with epoxy to a piece of copper, attaching them to the dowel or handle with a small automotive hose clamp. Sam stretched his skin with one hand and tattooed with the other. Stephanie helped him stretch sometimes and she tattooed the places he couldn't reach. The process was very painful, especially on the inner thigh. He only did the lower part of his body with the traditional-style tools, the rest by machine. When it is complete, the tattoo will cover most of Sam's body. Right now his legs are about half finished. He still has a lot of black to fill in, but he should be finished by the end of 1999 – if he can find the time. He is increasingly in demand to tattoo others in the community, mostly with arm bands, the most popular design although the band itself isn't traditional. He's using traditional designs from *tapa* (barkcloth) and other sources to create the bands and on women he does a lot of ankle bands and turtles and fish. Stephanie has bands on both her ankles, a dolphin on her stomach, and the 'Free Iupeliauro Iosefa Pauga' design on her back.

Sam finished talking about his life and heritage and why more and more young Tongan men want to wear the traditional tattoo, grabbed another beer, and said: 'So, what is it you want to know?' He looked at Billy, moving his expert eye over the young Maori's own tattoo, and then at me. 'Got any work on you? I can do you now, if you like. An arm band maybe? If you can stand it.'

Sam and Billy laughed. 'No thanks,' I said, 'I've had one done and that's enough.'

'Let's see,' Sam said and I rolled the sleeve of my T-shirt up to reveal a tattoo on my right shoulder. 'Hey, I like it,' he added, looking at the design, 'nice work.'

'So what can you tell me about Jonah and his uncle? I'm writing a book about Jonah's life and Billy says you may be able to help.'

'Yeah, sure,' he said, 'and Stephie here can tell you a bit as well. She knows the guy who did it and her grandfather is the guy who was going to tattoo Lomu.'

I looked at Billy. 'Yeah,' he said, 'the same guy who did me. Me and Stephie are blood related.'

Sam's young Maori wife allegedly had some kind of relationship with Pauga, although she was reluctant to talk about it and Sam didn't want to at all, probably because Stephanie was only a young teenager when Pauga last walked the Otara streets as a free man. 'It doesn't matter anyway,' she sighed, 'because he'll probably be dead this time next year.'

The word on the street in Otara is that Pauga has a price on his head. When he is released from prison and deported from New Zealand to Samoa there will be a certain Tongan assassin waiting to avenge the killing of Jonah Lomu's uncle and cousin. 'There are some people who have been waiting a long time to get even with Pauga,' Sam said. 'Vengeance, like love or hate, is a long time dying.'

Fair enough, I thought, but what I didn't understand is why Stephanie has 'Free Iupeliauro Iosefa Pauga' tattooed on her back, apart from the fact that she may or may not have had some kind of relationship with the Otara killer. 'He's not innocent, is he,' I said. 'He did it, didn't he?'

'Oh yeah,' Sam said, 'but it was an act of self-preservation. The Tongan gang led by Jonah Lomu's uncle had a contract out on Pauga. They were going to kill him, and had already done some bad things to Pauga's friends.'

'Like what?' I asked.

'Rape, torture, extortion, you name it, they did it,' he said. 'It was a gang war with the Tongan and Samoan gangs fighting over territory and the right to control organized crime in the area, including the supply of narcotics and weapons.'

It's virtually impossible to get a look at the file on the man who hacked Jonah Lomu's uncle to death ten years ago, and people in Otara and Mangere who know the convicted killer or knew his victim are reluctant to talk about it. With the exception of Sam and Stephanie and Billy, most of the people I met were either too afraid or too involved to dig up the past. Why, because the threads of the lives of those involved in the shocking gangland incident on that autumn day appear to be entangled deep in the roots of both the Samoan and Tongan communities in South Auckland.

It was on 30 April 1988 that Iupeliauro Iosefa Pauga, a Western Samoan, killed Tongan David Fuko with a sharpened machete, and then tried to decapitate the corpse. He nearly severed the arm of another man and attacked a third but missed. He was part of a group of Samoans who hunted down a group of Tongans at the Otara town centre in apparent retaliation for an earlier incident. He and four others were ordered to be deported after the trial, but for years Pauga's lawyers have been fighting to allow him to stay in New Zealand. At the time of writing, Pauga was due to be paroled within days and that is why I believe people in Otara and Mangere were reluctant to comment. 'By the time your book comes out,' Billy told me, 'Pauga could be dead.'

In May 1998, Pauga's appeal against deportation was

rejected by the Court of Appeal. A week later Crown solicitor Mark Woolford told me that Pauga could appeal against the decision to the Court of Appeal, but did not know if he would. 'The New Zealand Immigration Service won't wait for any appeal anyway,' Woolford added, 'and when he is paroled, which I believe is fairly soon, they will just take him straight from the prison to the aircraft.'

Pauga had wanted his deportation order declared invalid by the High Court and sought a review of a refusal of an application for citizenship. The deportation order was in force but could not be executed while he appealed to the Deportation Review Tribunal, but nothing more was needed after that appeal was turned down for the deportation order to be activated. It has always remained in force, so his permanent residence was subject to that. What the judge was saying in effect was that Pauga wasn't entitled to be in New Zealand indefinitely because he had already been served with a deportation order. The irony is that if he had made his application for citizenship before he was served with the deportation order, he would have had to have been granted it.

In the end the judge threw out one of Pauga's claims of bias and predetermination on the part of Graeme Lee, a former minister of internal affairs. Lee was reported to have said Pauga was a degenerate and despicable killer who should be deported, and later that Pauga was wasting his time applying for citizenship.

Pauga's future is uncertain and Billy could be right. You could now be reading about a man who doesn't exist, just as David Fuko no longer exists. One thing is certain though, the slaying turned Jonah Lomu from a life in gangs. Like his parents Semisi and Hepi, Jonah would rather not talk about it, although he admits: 'When I lost my uncle I knew I was either going to end up like him or behind bars.'

'Do you think that's true?' I asked Sam. 'Do you think Lomu would have ended up in jail or even worse, dead like his uncle?'

The tattoo artist thought for a moment, took another swig of Export Gold, and said: 'Maybe. From what I've heard, Jonah looked up to his uncle as some kind of role model. Fuko's lifestyle, you know, the macho gang thing, must have appealed to a young kid like Jonah. He was a bit of a tough guy himself you know. Did he tell you that he used to fight all the time?'

'Yes Sam, he did,' I said. 'He admits that he went off the rails, lost control of his life for a while. He became very violent and was starting to drift into the gang scene. But his mother Hepi insists that a lot of what is said about Jonah's past is just hype, and I have to admit that Mangere and Otara are not the same dangerous mean streets that I read about before I arrived in New Zealand.'

'Things have changed around here, but it's still a dangerous place,' Billy said. 'And I know for a fact that Jonah was in danger of following his uncle to the grave. He was already ankle deep in the shit that Foku was involved in and by the time he was 15 or 16 I reckon he'd have become just like his uncle.'

Lomu, or so the story goes, was spending more and more time in Otara in the months leading up to the incident that saw his uncle beheaded and cousin bleed to death. After their murder he allegedly vowed to get even with Pauga and the other members of the Samoan gang involved in the killing. Lomu won't admit to that but according to Stephanie, Fuko had some kind of hold over Lomu and it was he who first suggested that the young Tongan be tattooed as a sign of his new-found manhood. 'He saw potential in Jonah,' she said. 'Potential as a gang member. With his natural strength and speed Lomu would have been useful to have around. At the age of 13 he could handle other guys twice his age, and he feared no one. God only knows what would have happened to him had his mother not sent him away.'

She's probably right, only God knows that, and as I left Stephanie, Sam and Billy drinking Export Gold in the flat close to the killing floor where inter-racial tension exploded right in the face of two members of the Lomu 'family', my thoughts turned to Wesley College and the start of the rest of Jonah Lomu's life – the time in between death in Otara and life as an All Black.

8 JUGGERNAUT

**In the fell clutch of circumstance,
I have not winced or cried aloud:
Under the bludgeonings of chance
my head is bloody, but unbowed.**

William Ernest Henley

There is much truth in the 1996 advertising campaign of Jonah Lomu's sponsor, Reebok. It shows Lomu's unsmiling face with Reebok's logo cut into his left eyebrow. Below the intimidating face is a personalized number plate, J LOMU, and the words: 'Remember this plate. It's the plate of the truck that has just run you down.' Many players in addition to Tony Underwood and Mike Catt can relate to that. But long before the England pair's 1995 World Cup embarrassment highlighted why a New Zealand Prime Minister said his country should do everything it could to keep Lomu in union, and long before Leeds and Wigan wanted him and the Dallas Cowboys offered him $9 million to play American football for them, Jonah Lomu had earned the nickname 'Juggernaut'.

Reebok were right to hang a warning below his granite chin, because ever since Jonah Lomu learned how to run with a rugby ball the game has been scraping players off the pitch in the wake of his thundering boots.

At Wesley College, the school where he had his first introduction to rugby, several unfortunate boys, unlucky enough to be handed the task of trying to stop him, ended up on the casualty list, steamrollered by a young teenager with the power and speed of someone twice his age. It was not until his fourth year at school that he switched codes from league to union, where he played a variety of positions, including lock and flanker, but his searing pace – he ran the 100 metres in 10.87 seconds – marked him out for a place on the wing. It was there that he became the youngest player to appear for the All Blacks when he was picked to face France in 1994, aged just 19 years and 45 days. Crucially, though, had it not been for the dedicated staff of Wesley College, Lomu's fate could have twisted in another direction; his introduction to rugby might never have happened or might simply have failed to launch the career of a superstar. Perhaps even more significantly, Lomu could have pursued a career in athletics instead.

Now, the best part of a decade after graduating from Wesley and becoming a sporting legend, Lomu insists that he was 'born to play rugby'. In hindsight it's easy to say, but it could have been so different, and Lomu admits: 'During the first two or three years at Wesley I wanted to participate in as many different sports as possible. I was right into sport, all sport: athletics, table tennis, rugby. I enjoyed sprinting and for a while believed that was my calling, not rugby.' The coaches at Wesley felt the same way, before it became apparent that Lomu was more brilliant at rugby than the other sports at which he was merely outstanding. On the 100 metres track Lomu was stopping the clock at under 12 seconds virtually from day one. When he started smashing the 11-second barrier people started to talk. He was breaking school records in several other track and field events as well. Suddenly everyone was talking about the kid from Mangere – the one who had been plucked from the gutter and a life of crime and possible death.

For Hepi Lomu, Jonah's promising start to his new life was a dream come true. He settled in quickly. The violent temper and arrogance that fuelled the problems which plagued his last days as a potential thug on the streets of Mangere and Otara began to disappear, although he didn't become an angel overnight. But he was in the perfect environment to receive divine assistance in the exorcising of the demons that threatened to take him down the same hellish path on which his uncle and cousin had met their horrible fate only months earlier.

Wesley College is a Christian multi-racial school affiliated to the Methodist Church of New Zealand and has a special obligation to provide education for students of Maori or Pacific Island descent, and orphans or otherwise disadvantaged students. It aims to provide an environment in which students of all races can receive their education and learn to live and work together in harmony. This spirit of peacefulness had a profound impact on the young and troubled Lomu. Instead of existing in some kind of urban war-zone where race is an excuse for violence and death, Lomu found himself learning the haka with other, different, Polynesian Islanders, many of whom had arrived from the same difficult backgrounds, some also bearing the scars of teenage conflict on their young bodies and in their hearts and minds. Located at Paerata near Pukekohe, 35 miles south of Auckland, not far from Lomu's Karaka Park mansion, Wesley is a school with approximately 400 students from 11 to 17 years of age, both day and boarding and belonging to various cultural groups: Maori, Tongan, Samoan and Melanesian. All classes are open to all students so that the language and cultures of the Pacific can be shared and appreciated. Wesley gave Lomu an open mind and shut the door on his troubled past, although trouble of a different kind was waiting for him further on up the road that would eventually take him to the heights of rugby union.

Lomu spent the best part of four years at Wesley College and by the time he switched codes in his final year Ross Cooper, a pivotal force in New Zealand rugby, knew he was looking at a potential All Black. Cooper, then the coach at provincial side Counties and now a key member of John Hart's All Black coaching staff, was overwhelmed by Lomu's natural ability. In an interview for the South African *Weekly Mail & Guardian* in the summer of 1994, Cooper said: 'Never in all my rugby coaching career have I seen such a natural talent. Jonah Lomu, with his weight, his skills, his handling and his build is unbelievable.' By this time Lomu had begun his last teenage year and had successfully completed the transition from league to union, although he still wasn't established as an out and out winger. He played for Counties Under-16s and then for Counties Secondary Schools and in 1992 and 1993 earned a place in the New Zealand Secondary Schools as a backrow forward. Then came the bugle call from the national selectors and a place in the New Zealand Sevens side. The 1994 All Black trials and his debut against the French were a natural extension of the education.

The previous summer, Cooper, a level-headed and straight-talking rugby man not prone to imprudence or exaggeration, had predicted that within five years Lomu would become a 'superstar'. It was completely out of character for Cooper but for once in his life he felt justified in making such a bold statement. Sticking his neck out for Jonah Lomu was not so much a risk, more a solid investment. Cooper was so sure of Lomu's future that he never feared for a moment his words would come back to haunt him. The only thing Cooper got wrong was the timescale; it would take Lomu only two years to fulfil his destiny. Cooper also made the mistake of saying that Lomu would probably end up as a backrow forward and not a winger, although later in an interview for the *New Zealand Herald* he said: 'Jonah has the ability to play virtually anywhere he wants and be the best on the park. He is a player of strength, class and vision and he's not even twenty. He is still young so he needs support, but if he is handled right and gets his confidence up he can be a superstar. He will surely be a star in the 1999 World Cup, maybe sooner, but one day Jonah Lomu will certainly be a household name.'

Lomu was 18 years old when he played his first game for Counties. Cooper had been asked by the selectors to try Lomu on the wing as opposed to the backrow and it proved a difficult experience for the young Wesley College graduate. 'Playing on the wing was the hardest thing for me,' he recalled. 'It's all very well having the ball in your hands, but you've still got to know what to do with it, and I didn't have a clue in those early days.' Being a South Auckland boy, it was a special feeling for Lomu to play at Pukekohe Park, the home of Counties Manukau rugby club, not far from Wesley College. It must be one of the most peaceful settings for a rugby ground I have ever visited. Pukekohe Park is open on three sides with grassy banks and lines of evergreen trees surrounding the playing area, but on match days the place is a cauldron of colour and noise. 'It's home to me,' Lomu said. 'They are an awesome crowd and really get behind their players. It's what makes playing there so great.'

But, nevertheless, it took a while for Lomu to settle into the role handed to him by Cooper on the instructions of the New Zealand Rugby Football Union selectors; in fact it took Lomu a while to appreciate playing for Counties at Pukekohe Park. The young player may have dreamt about such a moment all his life, but his initial reaction to it was one of vertigo, mild panic even, of staring out into a stadium filled with noisy, expectant fans and thinking how he couldn't afford to blow it. Glimpsing a momentary hint of fear in his young player, Cooper told Lomu, with a certain amount of firmness in his voice, 'Just get in there and play as you know how to, you'll soon get into it.' It was easier said than done and for his first few outings in the red and white Counties shirt Lomu was knocked black and blue. He'd receive the ball and start to run but he lacked experience and tactical knowledge; the beginning of his learning curve was more of a gauntlet and terribly uncertain. One thing is certain, though, pursuing a career in sprinting would have been far less painful.

'It was tough,' he recalls, 'the players were a lot more physical and I was out there in an unfamiliar position and because Ross Cooper was the kind of coach who earned the players' respect and never demanded it, I never had a problem when he asked me if I'd move to the wing. It was very different and very difficult but I got a lot of help from the experienced guys such as Errol Brain, who led the team by example – he was inspirational to me. Peter Fats was a legend, captain of Western Samoa. He was a great morale-builder, always laughing – laughed when we were up, laughed when we were down.'

But there were times when Lomu must have felt like crying. Opposing players, fuelled by some base desire to baptize with fire, enjoyed breaking Lomu in. He was the new kid on the block, and one who by all accounts was destined for great things. On more than one occasion Lomu was hit hard before he even got the ball, although he laughs off stories that he was ready to throw in the towel. 'That's rubbish,' he says. 'I loved it because I am the kind of guy who thrives on physical contact. It's not easy to explain, but right from my younger days I always believed I was born to play rugby, to have the ball in my hands. Same thing with Counties. I was young and inexperienced but I knew I was meant to be there.'

It was a crude rite of passage, but the general consensus among the New Zealand press was that here was a star in the making. The experts compared notes and were, give or take a few doubts, united in their praise. Before the end of his first season at Pukekohe Park (now Steelers Stadium) Lomu had proved himself capable of more than holding his own. What seemed unique was that he appeared to have no fear, he was so self-assured, so determined. In many ways he is a paradox because off the field Jonah Lomu is not so self-assured or determined. The enthusiasm which he was beginning to generate among his supporters seemed a world removed from the darker realities that gripped his parents before his enforced escape from the violence of Mangere and Otara. At least the brutality of the game that now dominated his life could not easily destroy him, unlike the rival gangs that murdered his uncle and cousin, although he had yet to encounter John Kirwan – the legend and All Black enforcer.

For a long time the memory sent a shiver down Lomu's spine. If he was going to be tested further, what better than to face Kirwan, a man with enough testosterone to keep alive the myth that some All Blacks really do eat barbed wire for breakfast. 'I had to mark JK in my first All Black trial,' Lomu said. 'It gave me nightmares before the game. I'd heard all the stories about how tough and how strong and how quick he was and I didn't know what to expect. It was hard enough playing in a position I really knew nothing about, but on top of that I was up against the All Black great of the wing position.'

When I saw Kirwan score a 30-metre try in a 1990 Bledisloe Cup match at Christchurch's Lancaster Park, I knew I had experienced one of those rare life-changing moments, like the day my father took me to my very first big FA Cup game at Villa Park in 1977 – the day I became hooked on football. As Kirwan ran like an express train and his speed ripped apart the defence of Tim Horan and David Campese I became hooked on rugby too; at the age of 25, I was blown away by his overwhelming speed and strength and I certainly wouldn't have wanted to be in Lomu's boots on the day he faced JK – although that too was a life-changing moment and it shaped Lomu's career, albeit painfully.

John Kirwan was born on 16 December 1966 in Auckland, a day to remember for New Zealand rugby. At 6ft 4in and packed with athletic muscle, the desperately good-looking son of a butcher, cut through opponents with the surgical force of his father's meat cleaver and broke records with the same passion with which he broke hearts. His union career speaks for itself; sensational is the word that comes to mind. Sixty-three Tests and 35 tries – top Test try-scorer in New Zealand rugby history – for the All Blacks from 1984 to 1994; 96

games and 67 tries for New Zealand in all representative matches. And his rugby league career is equally outstanding: 35 games and 13 tries for the Auckland Warriors from 1995 to 1996 – top try-scorer with 10 tries in 1996. Kirwan left school at the age of 16 and became an apprentice butcher at his father's shop. He said about the shop: 'I used to like cleaning the window so I could check out the office girls walking past on their way to work. Chopping meat and perving at the same time was a skill I never quite mastered and I often cut my fingers trying to combine the two.'

Unfortunately for Lomu, Kirwan only had one thing on his mind on the day of the young Tongan's All Black trial and that was winning. All Blacks thrive on physical contact, both during games and at training. They make sure their presence is felt. Lomu felt Kirwan's presence all right, but he reacted badly and it almost cost him his All Black debut. 'I was a rookie and knew nothing,' he admits. 'I did not know how to take this physical contact stuff in training. I took it the wrong way and back then I just thought they didn't want me in the same side.'

Apart from being very green on the field, Lomu kept to himself and didn't say anything. Kirwan and company thought he was being arrogant when in reality he was confused. 'In hindsight I should have played my natural game,' Lomu added. 'But I could not forget about the pressures and what everyone was saying. Some of the older players, especially Sean Fitzpatrick, helped a lot, but at the time I really didn't know how to take things – things done the All Black way – and on top of that I was really conscious of my defensive weaknesses.'

These were later exposed against the French in the summer of 1994 when Lomu became the youngest All Black of all time. His debut in the first Test on 26 June at Christchurch was disappointing not so much for his own personal performance, which consisted of a couple of strong runs and not much else, but for the overall movement of the team, which saw the All Blacks thumped 22–8. Still, Lomu struggled, especially when the French forced him to turn and chase the ball. His bulk took on the shape of an oil tanker, quick when going forward but taking a long, long time to slow down and turn.

Lomu's selection against France came, in his own words, 'right out of the blue', following his courageous but nevertheless ordinary All Black trial, although Sean Fitzpatrick commented at the time that 'he's a natural with a big future'. Lomu himself wasn't so optimistic. 'I did a lot of things wrong during the trial and the last thing I expected was to be picked the next day to be an All Black. There was lots of hype about being the youngest Test player ever for New Zealand, but to be honest the age factor never even crossed my mind. I was selected to do the job, and that's where my focus was.'

It's not entirely true that Lomu did not dwell for at least one moment on the age factor. It gave him a few anxious moments as the hype surrounding his unprecedented arrival on the international Test scene had raised unrealistic expectations among the New Zealand sporting public, and it was because of this pressure that he sought the advice of teammate and fellow winger Jeff Wilson, who had been only a few months older than Lomu when he first played for the All Blacks. Wilson told him: 'Forget about it. Records are for the media to worry about, you just enjoy it.'

Lomu didn't, not even a little bit. After the first Test against France in Christchurch he had mixed feelings, and they did not include a sense of enjoyment, more a mix of pride and bitter disappointment. 'I wasn't happy,' he recalled. 'I was an All Black for the first time. That was great so I felt very proud, but the team had lost and I was not thrilled about my own performance so the strongest feeling was bad. Nobody could ever accuse me of being the greatest loser on earth.'

The second Test against the French in Auckland seven days later on 3 July also ended in defeat for the All Blacks. The final result was 23–20 to France, not as bad as the Christchurch deficit but still a bitter pill to swallow, especially for Lomu who suffered the same fate as he had on his debut the previous week. The French, having successfully exploited Lomu's deficiencies in Christchurch, did so again in his home city, only this time they made him look worse than he actually was. 'They went out knowing exactly what they were going to do,' he said. 'They exposed me and showed up my positional and defensive weaknesses.' In fairness New Zealand probably should have won. Their overall movement was better than that of France and they showed more fighting spirit, but they came unstuck largely thanks to one awful moment of indecision by Lomu. During a crucial point in the match he had to make a split-second choice who to tackle during a French move deep in their own half. He got it completely wrong and the moment will live with him forever. 'In the end I didn't take anyone,' he said, 'and they scored at the other end of the field. I still think about it sometimes.'

During this time, when he was learning the All Black trade the hard way, although that to a certain extent is the only way, Lomu was being watched. James Small, Lomu's opposite number in the green and gold of South Africa's Test side, studied his performance in both Test matches against France and came to the conclusion that maybe Lomu was not as good as people were making out. It was the first time since he had arrived in a blaze of potential glory on the New Zealand rugby scene that another Test player had publicly undermined Lomu's worth. Small had done his homework and his criticism was not without substance. 'Of course he's a big boy but I wasn't impressed with him against the French,' Small told a reporter from the *Weekly Mail & Guardian*. 'He looks incredible with the ball in his hands, his attacking skills are very good, he's still a hell of a player to face, but Test rugby demands a lot more than that, and from what I've seen he is lacking in certain crucial areas. What you've got to remember is that if you are six and a half feet from the ground then you are six and a half feet from the ball and that can be a problem for him. It may be virtually impossible to stop him on your own if he runs straight at you, but I've got a feeling that Jonah Lomu is not going to have it all his own way. There is more to rugby than just brute force and speed. I'd love to play against him next week but they'll probably drop him after the mistakes he made against France.'

Small's words returned to haunt Lomu twice; on the eve of the Test against South Africa in Wellington a week after the second Test against France, and during the final of the 1995 World Cup when Small's wish finally came true. Small was right, Lomu wasn't selected for the Wellington Test, and the decision became a turning point in the 19-year-old winger's career. He said: 'Not being picked to play against South Africa wasn't really a big letdown. I could see where the selectors were coming from and I knew I had to sort myself out.

'Not just the rugby bit, but more just getting away from the game for a while, spending more time with my mates and getting my head together. I was also at the union/league crossroads. I had a lot of league people – coaches, scouts etc – in my ear. It was decision time.' And that is how Lomu ended his first season as an All Black. The Auckland defeat by France would be his last Test match before the 1995 World Cup and that, he thought, could either make or break his dream.

9 WELCOME TO HELL

It's a freight train a comin' a ball clutched to his chest, the other huge mitt dealing out right handers, the beautifully chiselled abdomen held high and straight, the poise and balance perfect, the oak-trunk thighs pumping out their terrifying 'take me if you can' routine.

Saturday Star, Johannesburg

It was a long time coming, 328 days to be exact, but for Lomu it was worth the wait. His first full international match since the Auckland defeat by France in July 1994 would be the All Blacks' World Cup opener against Ireland in Johannesburg, South Africa. The date – 27 May 1995 – will go down in history as the day the rugby world at large truly discovered Jonah Lomu. Of course, rugby league clubs had been chasing him for two years, ever since his special talents were unleashed on an unsuspecting England Schools at Dunedin, a city in the south-east of New Zealand's South Island famous for its Scottish-Maori heritage. The result was England's heaviest defeat in history – a 52–5 humiliation – with Lomu scoring two tries, much to the delight of Dunedin's New Zealand Scots, but if the 20-year-old All Black was to prove himself, beyond a shadow of a doubt, as a truly world-class player the third World Cup was the acid test.

The painful memory of his first and only Test matches, when All Black coach Laurie Mains rushed him into the June and July 1994 Tests against France in Christchurch and Auckland, remained. Then, dogged by inexperience and a lack of confidence, Lomu was starved of the ball and scarcely featured in attack. His defensive naivety was also exposed and, as Springbok winger James Small predicted, Lomu was dropped after the second Test. Six months later he was drafted into the New Zealand squad at the Hong Kong Sevens and was one of the best players of the tournament as the Kiwis defeated Australia in the final. This and a commanding and timely performance in the All Blacks trial – when he scored two tries – which clinched his World Cup place, eased Lomu's fears of further failure, although not sufficiently to put him completely at ease.

Still conscious of his size, which had prompted him to experiment with playing wing-forward in between the second French Test and the Hong Kong Sevens, Lomu remained unconvinced of his ability to live up to the huge expectations of the sporting public, both back home in New Zealand and in South Africa. What he could not grasp in particular was the overwhelming reality of his pulling power as a major interna-tional sports star. He had remained loyal to his unfashionable province, Counties Manukau, and continued to enhance his already glowing reputation as an outstanding club player in New Zealand. He had also proved himself as a brilliant exponent of the sevens game, but as far as Test rugby as an All Black was concerned he had only two mediocre performances under his belt. In his mind, which frequently drifted back to the Christchurch and Auckland tests of 1994, he could not accept that someone of his limited experience, just turned 20, could become a millionaire overnight if he turned to rugby league or American football.

But it was a fact. As the All Blacks prepared to face Ireland in their opening game of the 1995 World Cup, with Lomu primed as potentially the most devastating weapon in their deadly armoury, the young Tongan – less than seven years out of the South Auckland 'ghetto' and only three years out of school – was being stalked by men with open chequebooks. The Dallas Cowboys, one of the wealthiest sports clubs in the world, were ready to invest around $9 million in a player whose natural attributes of speed and strength were still offset by complete inexperience. Auckland Warriors, New Zealand's foremost rugby league club, had already put their money on the table, offering Lomu a three-year £1.4 million deal, incorporating guaranteed personal sponsorship and endorsement opportunities. And representatives of Wigan, then British rugby league champions, were in the bidding process, allegedly with a package deal worth in excess of £3 million.

To cap it all the stout, intimidating figure of Peter Moore, executive of the Sydney Super League side Canterbury Bankstone and affectionately known as 'The Bulldog', was also keeping an eye on Lomu, and his money spoke so loudly that those within the All Blacks' inner circle, including coach Laurie Mains and a few of the elite NZRFU officials, feared they would lose Lomu after the World Cup. One NZRFU selector told me: 'At the time Lomu's name was at the top of every hit list from here to Texas. At the 1995 Hong Kong Sevens there were scouts from every Super League club I could mention and the Dallas Cowboys had half a dozen of their top guys over as well. They were all there to watch Jonah and yet, incredibly, he didn't understand what all the fuss was about. The only thing in Jonah's mind, before the 1995 World Cup, was proving he was good enough to be an All Black. Everyone knew he was, except Jonah.'

Unfortunately for Ireland Lomu felt equally determined as he lined up with the All Blacks for his first international in almost 12 months. Fifteen days earlier he had celebrated his twentieth birthday, but incredibly Lomu had already begun to feel as though time was slipping away from him, at least as an All Black. It was a ridiculous thing to imagine, especially as only 11 months earlier he had entered the history books as the youngest ever All Black, but it made him determined to exorcise the ghosts of the French Tests of 1994. For this experience too had become slightly distorted in his young mind. The only thing he had been guilty of in his two matches against the French was inexperience, although it seemed a whole lot worse to him. For the Irish, however, this was the worst possible news; facing a 6ft 5in 18 stone guided missile with something to prove is not the best way to start a World Cup.

Despite the doubts in his mind, returning to international rugby after the best part of a year was a special moment for Lomu. 'I was pulling on the black jersey again – what a feeling,' he later recalled. 'Our coach Laurie Mains got me fired up: "Take no prisoners, Jonah, have a crack. If you want to try something from your own goal-line ... go for it." '

He did, much to the delight of the handful of rugby league chairmen who had flown to the opposition's World Cup with the intention of bankrupting the whole of Lancashire and Yorkshire to buy him, and the three American money-men – representing the Dallas Cowboys, New York Giants, and San Francisco 49ers – one of whom wanted to see if it was true that Lomu can jump so high that he can clap his hands above a rugby crossbar. He can, although the Texan in question never got to see it. He did see Lomu score two tries in a 43–19 victory over Ireland, and the runs he made on those and on other occasions were quite incredible. His sheer power was overwhelming, especially during his unforgettable 50-yard run when he smashed past four brave Irish tackles before giving his flanker Josh Kronfeld a try.

It was significant, and a fact not lost on the watching scouts, that Ireland did very well for the first 20 minutes because, in the whole of that time, New Zealand did not give Lomu the ball. But as soon as they did he drove past three men with an incredibly athletic and powerful stride and put Walter Little clear away on the left. All Little had to do was keep in the field of play and run round behind the posts but he was careless enough to put a foot in touch with no defender near him. Lomu was not impressed, but just as Ireland wing Richard Wallace reminded his team-mates, 'For God's sake don't let him get the ball,' Kronfeld orchestrated a devastating move. The All Blacks worked the ball out to Lomu who did just as he had done before – but with one difference. This time, having brushed aside three Irish defenders as if they did not exist, he himself cruised round to score near the posts and Andrew Mehrtens kicked the goal.

Those two runs by Lomu had been made in the space of five minutes and he scored again at the beginning of the second half. It could have been worse for Ireland because Lomu was not firing on all cylinders, even though he was head and shoulders above most other players on the pitch. Nevertheless, on the day Kronfeld and Mehrtens and the veteran Frank Bunce played with more class. Afterwards the Irish wing Wallace admitted: 'If Lomu's only warming up then I'm glad we had him first. We were definitely the guinea pigs trying to work out how to stop him. He's the biggest player I've ever had to mark; he's positively super-human, and to think that he's only here to make up the numbers.'

That statement is not entirely accurate, although Wallace had a point. Had it not been for an injury to Eric Rush, Lomu may not have got his chance and he admitted this during a candid interview with a New Zealand newspaper reporter after the Ireland match. 'Had Rushy made it, I might not have,' he said. 'I wasn't initially selected in the World Cup training squad which was a major disappointment – a big setback for me and I didn't know what to think. It got me down but I tried to stay positive. Never say never is an attitude I try to maintain, because you never know what's around the corner.'

For Lomu that happened to be Taupo, the legendary All Black training camp from hell. With fire and brimstone burning at its core and snow-capped mountains towering at its centre, the Taupo and Tongariro region of New Zealand's North Island uneasily awaits further volcanic tantrums. For once Lomu found himself in a place more intimidating than himself and the intensity of it all almost brought him to his knees.

During the three-day camp, from 3 to 6 February 1995, All Black coach Laurie Mains wanted to determine the levels of fitness of his players and introduced saturation coaching, with the emphasis on drills and the basic techniques that would be required to play their World Cup game. Mains, a man who managed to evoke extreme passions throughout New Zealand while he was coaching the All Blacks from 1992 to shortly after the 1995 World Cup, had a reputation as a merciless trainer. After he ended his own All Black playing career, Mains picked up three teams that were down and out – Southern, Otago and New Zealand – and converted each one into a champion side playing brilliantly creative rugby. But at a price. Ask anyone who trained under Mains to remember what it felt like and invariably they come out with words like 'murderous' and 'ruthless'. At the Taupo pre-World Cup camp Mains was determined to put the All Blacks through the physical demands that would allow him to assess their courage, skill and rugby fortitude. These three days in 'hell' would show him which players had the qualities that would manifest at crucial times and allow the All Blacks to win Test matches. It was Mains' intention to give his players as many as eight hours a day of physically demanding work, not just through running and basic exercises but in re-creating match situations. Ross Cooper would later refer to the Taupo camp as 'brutality'.

It was extremely physical and demanding but it also built character and created unity, bonding the team. The players retained their spirit, if not always their humour. And the word got around that the All Blacks were really doing something special, so at the start of the day at Owen Delany Stadium as many as 500 people were watching the 'brutal' sessions, and by mid-afternoon that number had swelled to almost a thousand. Spectators were overwhelmed by the sheer intensity of Mains' training methods, especially the 'ball-breaking' sprints that rounded out the days. Mains, who must have been a professional torturer in another life, made his already exhausted players perform a series of 150-metre sprints – 22 of them to be precise – and some 60 or 70 down and ups, at the end of which they were so burnt out they could hardly walk off the ground. And yet, as the All Black coach pulled out of the stadium, fans could see players laughing and joking among themselves; these guys had come through a full day of strength-sapping confrontation drills, finishing off with gut-busting 150s – like playing four consecutive games of rugby – and still their spirit remained unbroken, with the exception of one or two individuals.

One target for special attention from Mains at the Taupo camp was Lomu. He had experienced the emotional extremes, inside a month, of debuting for, and then being dropped from, the All Blacks, but compared to the agony waiting for him at the Owen Delany Stadium the French experience was a picnic. It was during the Auckland camp in December 1994 that Mains sat with Lomu and explained that the selectors were promoting him to the main squad for Taupo in February. In the two months before Taupo, with the South African World Cup looming, Lomu was urged to put a huge amount of effort into fitness work and not to worry about anything else. Lomu obeyed orders but he became very anxious about the prospect of the three-day Taupo camp, and justifiably so.

Now Mains knew very well that Taupo would probably break Lomu and because he genuinely liked the young Tongan he was reluctant to put him through it, especially as the 1994 series had been so difficult for him. 'After the second Test against France in Auckland he was devastated,' Mains admitted, 'and we had to make a decision whether to persevere and risk a greater loss of confidence or explain what had happened and let him continue playing club rugby where he could apply the lessons learnt as an All Black. We felt if the hard work was put in, he could make it.' Mains still had his doubts though, mainly whether Lomu was capable of achieving the high aerobic levels required of an All Black. So it came down to a case of having to be cruel to be kind. Exposing Lomu to the 'brutality' of the Taupo regime was the only sure way of properly assessing the player.

The tests at Taupo during the three days in February 1995 revealed that Lomu's fitness levels did not match up to most of the others, given that the three-day camp was the most demanding training an All Black could wish to endure. Lomu was well off the pace, but he did demonstrate a high degree of determination. That, along with the injury to Eric Rush, is the reason why he ended up facing Ireland in Johannesburg three months later. Some of the senior members of the squad ran with him, offering encouragement, but Lomu found Taupo an almost distressingly difficult experience. By the time of the fourth training camp at Christchurch, only weeks before the World Cup, there were serious doubts as to whether Lomu would make the fitness levels required to play in South Africa. A poisoned leg didn't help, meaning he was unable to do as much work as the other players, although that may have been a blessing in disguise as Lomu was on his last legs anyway.

Mains and other members of the coaching staff, and several of the more senior players, spoke to Lomu between the Taupo and Christchurch training camps. Sean Fitzpatrick, especially, spent a lot of time with Lomu, encouraging him and offering to train with him, one on one, in Auckland as a means of boosting his fitness levels in an eleventh-hour bid to make the cut. But Lomu was becoming more and more disillusioned and anxious. Mains' uncompromising philosophy that he wanted only players who could hold up when exhaustion threatened late in a game, and that there was no place for those with mental or physical shortcomings, was hard to comprehend for a young man like Lomu who had found rugby effortless at school and who suddenly realized he was struggling to make the grade.

The All Black coach in fact believed he still had time to prepare Lomu, but wanted him, more than anything else, to confront the issue of his fitness – or lack of it – and understand that he had to do it if he was to make the World Cup. It was a shrewd psychological tactic by Mains, who never left anything to chance and intended to cover all his bases in the event of injury to other certain World Cup starters. In essence, Mains decided to keep pushing Lomu for as long as possible because deep down he believed that the All Blacks' chances of success in South Africa would improve with Lomu on board. He was proved right in the end, but had it not been for the twist of fate – or more precisely the strained groin – that deprived Mains of Eric Rush, Lomu's fitness levels would probably have been his downfall after all.

Lomu, according to Earle Kirton – one of Mains' coaches at the time – was 'beside himself with joy and relief' when he learned of his promotion at the expense of the injured Rush. 'He arrived at the final trial before South Africa absolutely fizzing,' Kirton said. 'It was a huge lift in morale for him.' So much so that Lomu's new-found enthusiasm almost cost one the All Blacks' best-ever tacklers, Paul Henderson, a night in casualty. The World Cup squad were doing drills at training, the ball carrier being required to run hard at players standing in a square holding tackle bags. Henderson, a ferociously hard tackler, had had no previous contact with Lomu, and when Lomu hit him, he landed six metres away. He was totally shocked and could not train properly for the rest of the day. Later, when Lomu hit another player, Richard Loe, his feet went a full 12 inches off the ground and he landed on his backside. It prompted Blair Larsen's famous quote: 'This guy makes Inga Tuigamala look like the tooth fairy.'

For the first time, Lomu was showing confidence and excitement about being with the All Blacks, although it wasn't until after his return to international rugby in the World Cup defeat of Ireland that he was able to relive the agony and ecstasy of those crucial few months between his post-France depression, the hell of Taupo, and his moment of realization that he was going to South Africa. It was as though the final whistle at the end of the All Blacks' opening World Cup match triggered some kind of emotional release, because for the first time in his career Lomu opened his heart, and what came out shaped the rest of his and New Zealand's World Cup.

It was American journalist Paul Brookes, a laid-back Auckland-born freelance rugby fanatic, who discovered that Lomu had seriously thought about quitting union after Taupo. Lomu spilled the beans a few hours after helping to destroy the Irish and the news sparked a renewed effort by league clubs to try and persuade Lomu to switch codes. NZTV's Television Three, Brookes discovered, had sparked the chain of events that almost led to Lomu leaving New Zealand and playing rugby league for an English club or American football for the Dallas Cowboys. The idea of Lomu switching sports completely and starting a new life in Texas seemed preposterous to some but after TV3 stated, strangely on their news rather than their sport segment, that he was no longer in contention for the World Cup team, and dropped a broad hint that his All Black career was under threat, Lomu seriously considered the option. Brookes, based just outside Dallas in Tyler, later revealed that the Cowboys went as far as drawing up a contract for Lomu after they heard, allegedly through a NZRFU insider, that he was planning to switch codes following the Television Three item.

By chance, both Laurie Mains and Lomu had their television sets tuned to TV3 when the story broke, three or four weeks before the injury to Rush opened the World Cup door for Lomu. Mains almost choked and could not believe what he was hearing. 'The report was without foundation and was totally irresponsible,' he said. 'It could have cost the All Blacks and rugby this talented player. We – the selectors – knew the game we were playing with Jonah. We were feeding him enough carrots to keep him coming forward. I was angry and distraught and immediately telephoned TV3 demanding a retraction and an apology to Jonah.'

Lomu was sitting in the lounge of his South Auckland home, with friends, when the news item appeared. 'It just hit me – splat!' he said. 'It was a huge shock. They said I was out of contention for the World Cup and appearing as a major news item like that, you had to presume there was a strong basis of truth there. I took it to heart. They were writing me off, and I just freaked out.'

Lomu went off the rails at that moment. He jumped up, put his jacket on and took off. For the next two days he hung out on the streets and in bars with his friends, trying to come to terms with what he had heard. 'It was obvious to me how Laurie Mains was thinking,' Lomu added. But he had had no communication at all with the All Black coach; in fact Mains and the NZRFU spent 48 frantic hours trying to reach Lomu and during that time he virtually made up his mind to quit. He admits that at that point he considered accepting one of the several offers he'd received from league clubs and the United States. 'It seriously crossed my mind,' he says. 'What held me back were friends like Eric Rush who said the best way to deal with a situation like that was to prove them all wrong.'

Ironically, Lomu was enormously grateful to Rush for his support at that time. He knew he could trust his fellow All Black, who maybe would not have been so understanding had he known that less than a month later he would lose his World Cup place. 'Eric told me to believe in myself, told me to stick to my guns; he really put my mind at ease. Thanks to him I'm right here playing for the All Blacks at the World Cup, and it makes me sick to think that because of something someone said on TV I almost walked out on rugby union.'

TV3 subsequently apologized to Mains and carried an on-air retraction; in explaining to Lomu that the NZRFU selectors were entirely innocent of the television item they had to declare their hand, letting him know they were planning to take him to the World Cup. 'It was definitely a crisis time in his career and a crisis time for New Zealand rugby. We came so close to losing him.'

So Mains had a right to look happy as he patted Lomu on the back after the All Blacks' opening World Cup match against Ireland. At least now Lomu could rake over the coals of his recent past without worrying so much about the future.

In an interview with an Auckland newspaper he admitted: 'Taupo nearly killed me, it was that bad. It was brutal and designed to sort out players who could survive anything. I was the worst there but I was determined to finish. I refused to give up and I didn't. I never gave up. I wasn't going to lie down for anyone, even if it meant having to crawl to the end of the session. My dream lay at the end of it. When I got named in the World Cup squad I was rapt, and now I have a chance to show everyone that I am up to it. I am hungry for success and I think I proved that today. I want to show the world I can score tries and defend. I want the world to see the real Jonah Lomu.'

And so did Wales. They were up next, after the Irish, and took an entirely different approach, claiming they not only had the measure of Laurie Mains' side but were relishing the prospect of taking Lomu down a peg or two. Alex Evans, the Welsh coach, said he was targeting New Zealand and could beat them, and he went further by declaring his players had the ability and athleticism to 'expose All Black weaknesses', and would be superior to them in the tight five. Evans did not enjoy eating his words afterwards but the All Blacks, especially Lomu, enjoyed making him do it. They obliterated the Welsh forwards in the opening 40 minutes, and so incensed were players like Sean Fitzpatrick and Mike Brewer at Welsh claims of forward dominance that, once they had the game in hand, instead of opening it up, they took it upon themselves to keep taking the Welsh on up front. They were determined to show them who was in charge. The All Blacks won easily, 34–9, but Fitzpatrick and Brewer were guilty of sabotaging Mains' tactical plan for the evening – for which they received a dressing down from the All Black coach the next day – and Lomu was denied the chance to slaughter Wales out wide.

'The Welsh tried the mental game with us – talking it up in the press, saying they could take us – but it backfired on them,' Lomu recalls. 'The talking stops when you get out on the track and the whistle goes. We did the job in the end, that's all that matters, although it became a bit of a personal crusade for Fitzy and Mike and I didn't score even one try which was obviously disappointing.'

Even so, Lomu was pleased with his overall performance in the opening two games in Johannesburg. He'd also just met his future wife, Tanya Rutter, although he didn't know it at the time. Nor did he realize that his next game, against Scotland, would be his best yet for the All Blacks, but in a white shirt – his least favourite colour.

An element of controversy surfaced in the run-in to the quarter-final against Scotland, both teams believing they were staying in the same Holiday Inn hotel. The Scots had been based in Pretoria throughout the pool play and were reluctant to move their base. It was the All Blacks who were in the right and Scotland had to move, which upset them. 'They were antagonistic,' Mains said. 'But the accommodation was determined by where you finished in your pool and that was that.'

Some heat was taken out of the situation when the All Blacks lost the toss and had to wear white jerseys to avoid clashing with the traditional dark blue of Scotland. Mains was happy with that situation because he believed it would help focus his players. It did, although Lomu wasn't entirely at ease with the change. He is superstitious about wearing the black jersey, but the way everything was going for him in South Africa his luck wasn't about to run out.

Organizational problems, however, continued to hinder the All Blacks' preparation for the quarter-final match. Only now it wasn't accommodation causing problems but the allocation of training slots at Loftus Versfeld in Pretoria. One of the World Cup rules was that teams could practise at the match venue 48 hours prior to a contest. Once again the All Blacks and Scotland tossed, because they both wanted to train at 10.30 a.m. Scotland won, meaning the All Blacks were given the 12 noon slot. But when they arrived, the Scots were still running. To avoid embarrassment Mains went back to the dressing room and instructed All Black liaison officer Jan Oosthuizen to clear the ground but despite his best efforts, 15 minutes later Scotland were still stubbornly occupying the Loftus Versfeld turf.

Mains and Oosthuizen came to the conclusion that the All Blacks were victims of Scottish 'mind games' and decided to retaliate with a game of their own. Mains explained the situation to his players and delivered the battle plan. They would emerge on to the field as a tight unit, walk straight through the first group of Scots they encountered and make their way to the far corner where the warm-up would commence. The All Black players loved it. Mains, following them out, soon realized that they had achieved a psychological blow when he saw the look on the faces of the Scotland players, who immediately packed up and left the stadium.

By the time the quarter-final came around the All Blacks were brimming with confidence and Scotland were still 'pissed off', according to Oosthuizen, setting the stage for what most neutrals believed would be a fight to the death. It was also to be an historic afternoon at Loftus Versfeld; Sean Fitzpatrick was making his 100th appearance for the All Blacks and, as a direct result of the outcome, Gavin Hastings his final international appearance. The Scotland captain had hoped his team might survive through to the World Cup final but the All Blacks were too strong, too quick, and too hungry for tries, especially Lomu who recalls: 'We were all aware of New Zealand's record against the Scots. Many of the players remembered Scotland as the team they'd put 50 points on at Murrayfield in 1993. None of us wanted out at the quarter-final stage, and we certainly didn't want to be remembered as the first All Black side to be beaten by Scotland. The year before I'd been labelled the youngest ever ex-Test player and I didn't need another tag.'

Lomu needn't have worried. Despite a brave Scotland performance the All Blacks won 48–30 with Lomu scoring his third try of the World Cup. Tanya Rutter had bet him if he scored a try he had to sign her initials in the air. Lomu was happy to oblige. 'There must have been something in the air that day,' he said. 'Some guy told me after the game he'd had £200 on me to run through Gavin Hastings. Was he a happy guy.' At the post-match press conference Hastings asked: 'He's a big bastard, isn't he?' referring to Lomu. 'I've never struck anything like him. The All Blacks are damned lucky they never have to tackle him!'

Lomu was happy, Tanya Rutter had a funny feeling that she'd met the man of her dreams, and the All Blacks were safely through to the semi-finals. There they would meet England who had surprised everyone by defeating the then reigning world champions Australia, thanks to a sensational dropped goal from Rob Andrew. So it was England, not the Wallabies, who stood between the All Blacks and a World Cup final appearance at Ellis Park, and the chance to slaughter a team he had been led to believe were a negative force in world rugby put a tingle in the gut of Jonah Lomu. Deep inside he knew something extraordinary was about to happen.

10 FAIRYLAND

A little man against a big one, and the
chances are in favour of the little one.
The cat has the best of it with a dog.
Goliaths are always vanquished
by Davids.

Victor Hugo, *The Man Who Laughs*

Of all the million and one things Tony Underwood could
have said to Jonah Lomu a week before the All Black-
England semi-final in Cape Town, he had to come out with
just about the only one capable of making the big man's blood
boil – a dig at his defensive skills. Nothing else, not even a low
blow aimed at his family, girlfriend or race, would have hit the
spot in quite the same way. Something inside Lomu snapped;
not a volatile snapping, more of a controlled explosion, but
nevertheless a reaction of vital force that would prove England's
downfall on 18 June 1995, shattering not only the dream of a
nation but also the pride of a band of men, many of whom still
have nightmares about the day that Lomu laid down the law.

The English, it is fair to say, have an unfailing knack of creating motivation for the opposition, and a good deal of the stimulus that charged the All Blacks at Cape Town could be sourced to Tony Underwood's remarkable comment, while in South Africa, to a newspaperman. 'Who's Jonah?' he asked. 'He hasn't marked anyone yet, probably because he can't defend.' It was either an incredibly naive statement or the England winger seriously underestimated the opponent he would oppose at Newlands. Coach Laurie Mains, always ready to turn a situation to the All Blacks' advantage, made sure Lomu was aware of Underwood's comment and gave him several reminders during the run-up to the semi-final. Come match day Lomu was as pumped up as he's ever been for a rugby match. Underwood had actually done Mains a big favour; if only the All Blacks could get that level of mental intensity into Lomu every time, the coach thought as prepared his side for their most important game in years.

To quote Sean Fitzpatrick, Lomu was 'really pissed off', so much so that he cut out Underwood's quote and stuck the clipping on the mirror in his hotel room. Every morning and every evening it was there, staring at him. 'By the time I faced Underwood out on the track I was bursting with adrenaline,' Lomu said. 'Each day I'd see the clipping and I'd say to myself, "Yeah, okay Tony, we'll get it on at the end of the week." There was plenty of talk in the media before the game, some good and some not so good. The English were saying how they could win; what they were going to do to different players. A lot of the talk was about me – all the stuff about being weak defensively. Tony Underwood was quoted as saying he believed he could run around me. I wanted to ram his words back down his throat.'

Left Lomu, on his international debut, challenged by Emile N'Tamack. (1st Test: New Zealand v France, Christchurch, 26 June 1994) *Colorsport*

Above Lomu escapes Rob Andrew during the 1995 World Cup semi-final in South Africa. (New Zealand v England, Cape Town, 18 June 1995) *Allsport*

Left World Cup Final: Springbok No. 15 Andre Joubet tries to stop Lomu during South Africa's victory over the All Blacks. (Johannesburg, 24 June 1995) *Colorsport*

Above Lomu, captain Sean Fitzpatrick and fellow winger Jeff Wilson celebrate winning the Bledisloe Cup. (Australia v New Zealand, Sydney, 29 July 1995) *Colorsport*

Right The All Black No. 11 in unstoppable mood. (1st Test: New Zealand v England, Carisbrook, 20 June 1998) *Colorsport*

Right Lomu marks his European debut with the first of two tries, to the delight of All Black captain Sean Fitzpatrick. (Italy v New Zealand, Bologna, 28 October 1995) *Allsport*

Left In action at Pukekohe Park, now known as Steelers Stadium, Manukau. (National Provincial Championship: Counties v Canterbury, 1995) *Photosport, New Zealand*

Right International and club team-mate Joel Vidiri congratulates Lomu on a successful comeback from illness. (National Provincial Championship: Counties v Otago, Pukekohe Park, Manukau, October 1997) *Photosport, New Zealand*

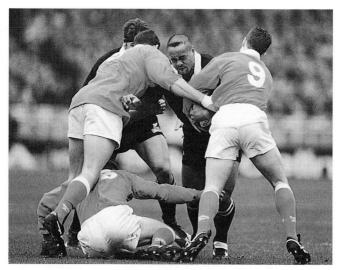

Above Lomu is tackled by Mike Voyle and Rob Howley during his international comeback. (All Blacks Tour: Wales v New Zealand, Wembley Stadium, 23 November 1997) *Allsport*

Above Lomu, No. 11, and his Auckland Blues team-mates pray after the match. (Super 12 Final: Auckland v Natal, Eden Park, Auckland, 25 May 1996) *Photosport, New Zealand*

Right With girlfriend Tanya Rutter. (Iewan Evans Testimonial: Llanelli, 21 November 1995) *Allsport*

Below Lomu, (4th right), introduced to South African President Nelson Mandela before the 1995 World Cup Final. (South Africa v New Zealand, Ellis Park, Johannesburg, 24 June 1995) *Colorsport*

Above Lomu (centre) performs the Haka after New Zealand defeated Fiji to win the gold medal in the rugby sevens competition at the XVI Commonwealth Games. (New Zealand v Fiji, Kuala Lumpur, 14 September 1998) *PA News*

Left The trademark No. 11 shaved in Lomu's right eyebrow, pre-1995 World Cup finals, South Africa. *Photosport, New Zealand*

Above Lomu with manager/agent Phil Kingsley-Jones during the
All Blacks UK Tour, 1997. *Photosport, New Zealand*

Below In relaxed mood and looking forward to starting his first
international match in over 15 months: All Blacks UK Tour, 1997.
Photosport, New Zealand

He did – metaphorically – and England probably deserved everything they got, especially after the way some of their players had acted following England's victory over the All Blacks at Twickenham in November 1993. 'Our players did not appreciate their gloating and complete lack of humility,' Mains claimed. Brian Moore's comment in his newspaper column, the day after the Twickenham match, that Fitzpatrick had called Victor Ubogu 'a black bastard', had remained lodged, like an irritating tick, under the skin of the All Black forward for the best part of two years. The appalling thing about Moore's statement was not what was said in the heat of the Twickenham match, because Fitzpatrick more than likely did say it, but the way Moore undermined the oldest and most respected unwritten rule; what happens on the rugby field, stays there. This has always been accepted practice and in this respect Moore was out of order. He broke that code. It meant he and Underwood would be special targets at Newlands.

Mains was a happy man. He had always wanted his All Blacks to take on England at the 1995 World Cup tournament in South Africa, and now, less than a week before it was going to happen, two of his most dangerous players were more determined and focused than they had ever been before a game of rugby, and the rest of the squad were also baying for blood. It wasn't just that England had dented All Black pride in 1993; the arrogance exhibited by many of the players and management afterwards had left a bitter taste in the mouth of Mains and his team. 'There were,' said the All Black coach, 'a good few survivors of that black day at Twickenham who longed for the opportunity to gain retribution.'

Lomu wasn't one of those but it didn't stop him from joining in the spirit of vengeance, especially now he had a score to settle himself. 'If there was a game the boys wanted to win,' he said, 'this was it. Everybody remembered the loss in '93 – there was still a lot of hurt, even within the guys who weren't in that side. I was still at school that year, but I remember clearly the look on guys' faces after losing to England. I didn't want to feel like that – not in the black jersey. No way!'

As Mains so delightfully put it, 'England had been an itch in the All Blacks' jock strap since the 15–9 defeat in November 1993', but there were other reasons for their enthusiasm for the semi-final pairing. One was that they all believed that the worst possible outcome for rugby was for England to triumph at the World Cup. 'England played awfully negative rugby throughout the Five Nations championship,' Fitzpatrick said, 'when they possessed a talented bunch of forwards who could have set the tone for a really open game.'

The All Blacks not only wanted to defeat England in Cape Town but in doing so wanted to demonstrate the exciting attacking options possible under the existing laws. What England didn't know was that as far back as February 1995, Mains and his players had plotted tactics specifically designed to neutralize them. The All Blacks had identified England as a top contender at the 1995 World Cup and Mains reasoned there was a strong chance his side would play them, or certainly a team employing similar tactics. Mains' thinking was that the All Blacks would be in a no-lose situation: what they were practising would work against any opponent, not just England.

So the All Blacks prepared techniques and tactics to combat England, several months before the start of the South

African World Cup, in the belief that only minor adjustments would be required for matches against other opponents. One of the major areas of concern for Mains was to avoid a repeat of their fate in 1993 when the British Lions and England had too often killed the All Blacks' forward play. It was obvious to him that if his players got into grappling situations the game would be slowed down to the opposing team's pace, as it was during the bitter Twickenham defeat. Mains knew that they could not afford to make that mistake in South Africa.

The game had to be played at All Black tempo so Mains devised a plan. It was simple but deadly and revolved around the pace and power of Lomu. After securing possession from controlled situations, they would commit their loose forwards, who almost always stayed in close, and then advance the ball to their wingers. The idea was to get the ball to either Lomu on the left or Jeff Wilson on the right as quickly as possible, knowing the skills of arguably the two best wingers in the game would be too much for Tony and his brother Rory Underwood who were not renowned for their courage.

This tactic was a direct focus of much of the work at the summer camps, especially Taupo, where, despite his fitness problems, Lomu looked unstoppable when he was released to run with the ball. But it was at Warkworth, in April – one month before the World Cup – after the All Blacks for South Africa had been selected, that Lomu and Andrew Mehrtens began practising the reverse kick tactic that would tear the heart out of England's game plan at Newlands. The pair spent hours at a time, drenched to the bone in torrential rain, practising the kick-off to the 'wrong' side, although no one would have guessed it as a vital tactic being refined for the semi-finals. Most of the time, to an outsider, it would have appeared that Lomu and Merhrtens were just fooling around. The All Blacks also spent a lot of time practising going forward aggressively into the other team's mauls to stop them, and once it was confirmed that England would be the opposition, the forwards worked more strenuously than ever before on moves to counter England's renowned powerful mauling, using the reserves as opponents. Mains figured that if a player drove in with the ball and the next two players to arrive went in with real force there would be no slowing down of the ball. It was all so simple, but that is the beauty of Mains' incisive thinking. He knew what was required to bury England in Cape Town and Lomu would play a big part in digging the hole.

England, after two days of rest and recuperation in Sun City following their removal of Australia as world champions, declined to be alarmed by the Lomu factor. Opposite the 118kg giant would be Tony Underwood, England's unrepentant and undersized winger, a mere stripling of 73kg and looking more and more like a small animal about to stray into the path of a truck. Reebok's famous Lomu advert was then still only a glint in the eye of some creative advertising executive but Underwood would certainly remember the plate of the truck that was about to run him over, and for a very long time.

For England's record-breaking captain Will Carling, though, Lomu would not be a direct problem, and because there was one sure way to cope with the hazard – or so he thought – Carling chose to worry about his bad stomach instead. He had been holed up under tight security with the rest of the England side in Sun City, nursing an abdominal complaint, basking in the still-warm glory of the quarter-final triumph over Australia, and momentarily allowing his thoughts to drift toward the rewards that victory over the All Blacks would bring. Still, Lomu was a factor worthy of an extra few minutes' debate during the England team meeting on their return from Sun City to Johannesburg, with Carling sticking comfortably to his theory: deny Lomu the ball in attack, put it behind him and make him turn in defence – no more hazard!

That, thought Carling, would help England reach the final and at the same time establish a national record of 11 consecutive international victories, having equalled the previous mark against Australia. The record had stood for more than 100 years and Carling couldn't wait to add another star to his already spectacular collection of merit marks.

There was just one problem; Mains' shrewd game plan virtually guaranteed that Lomu could not be denied the ball, let alone be made to turn in defence. Carling didn't know it but he was dreaming and the dream would soon turn into a nightmare as the terror-striking plate of the truck hurtling towards them came into view – 'J LOMU, remember this plate!'

England's luck was already running out, but still it took a major slice of luck that went New Zealand's way to really set the stage for what would be Lomu's greatest hour yet. The first break for Laurie Mains' All Blacks on the eve of the Newlands semi-final was a change in the weather. The depression which had soaked Cape Town midweek had moved east to lash Durban, almost causing the postponement of the South Africa–France semi-final. Cape Town, meanwhile, was basking in summer-like conditions; perfect for Lomu who is more effective when the going is good. Stroke of luck number two came when Sean Fitzpatrick won the toss and decided that his team would take the kick-off. The reverse kick, which

Lomu and Merhtens had been working on since April, could be employed. When the news got through to Lomu he burst into a huge grin: 'Hey, Fitzy,' he said, 'I can't wait to see the look on England's faces. Man, are they gonna be confused!'

The look on Tony Underwood's face was one of pure arrogance. Half Lomu's size and much less of a force, the England winger was hell bent on provoking the All Black No. 11. Maybe he had taken his brother Rory's pre-match hype to heart. 'I'm sure that Lomu will have been thinking about Tony running at him,' said Rory. 'And, in a one-on-one, I'd put my money on Tony.' That was all very touching and Rory may have had a point, if only a small one, because his brother was no mean winger and, rather like a bear-baiting terrier, Tony Underwood has tenacity.

'Tony winked at me during the haka,' Lomu recalled. 'He was up for it, but so was I. Many people believe there was lots of verbal aggro between him and me because of that, but there wasn't. When I'm doing the haka, I'm issuing a challenge. I guess that was Tony's way of accepting it. All I said was, "I'm gonna wipe that wink off your face, man." End of story.'

It was almost the end of Tony Underwood, although he still had a few minutes before his worst nightmare unfolded at Newlands. First, the final piece of Mains' deadly simple game plan had to be put into place and that involved a cunning act of trickery right in the middle of the Cape Town pitch. Mains had advised his players to remain huddled in midfield following the haka because there was usually a full minute before the referee signalled for the game to start. Mains feared that if his side lined up to the right as planned, the English players might, given too much time, suspect that something was going on, because kick-offs usually go left.

England fell for it and Mehrtens' reverse kick-off worked like a charm. Under pressure from Lomu, Will Carling knocked on, conceding the first scrum put-in to the All Blacks. You could see Carling turn and look around at his team-mates as if to say, 'Get ready for the first high ball towards their fullback,' but Mehrtens didn't kick, he passed, and in a flash the ball was in the hands of right winger Jeff Wilson who made good yardage. The All Blacks held the ruck long enough to allow England's powerful forwards to arrive, just as Mains had told them to, before quickly switching the attack left, out to Lomu. In truth it was a dreadful pass from fullback Glen Osborne, but Lomu retrieved it, swatted away Tony Underwood, and accelerated around Carling before trampling over the top of England full-back Mike Catt for a breathtaking try.

Suddenly, everything New Zealand warned that Lomu would do to England, he did. With 70 seconds on the clock, the All Blacks were in front by five points, and instead of resisting the temptation to engage England from the restart, which Mains had instructed them to do, they executed another onslaught. Mains, sitting in the grandstand to get a better overall view of the game, was a picture of mixed emotion. You could see him mentally willing his team to kick deep and force England to put the ball into touch, giving the All Blacks the throw-in to the lineout, but as soon as Walter Little was thrown the ball in his 22, Mains' eyes widened. Surely he wasn't going to launch an attack, was he?

The strategy of kicking deep from the restart to force an All Black lineout flashed across Little's mind. In that split second he could hear the words of his coach but, being the instinctive player that he is, Little decided to let England have it. Mains' eyes threatened to pop out of his head as the All

Black midfielder muscled past Jeremy Guscott before Osborne's blistering pace and Kronfeld's great support play produced another try, even more sensational than the first – one that was to claim the Famous Grouse trophy as the outstanding try at the 1995 World Cup. Two tries in four minutes, England were reeling on the ropes and Lomu was winding up one hell of a knockout punch.

He was so superior at one stage, as the All Blacks continued to stretch their advantage, that he could afford to dawdle against a defence in tatters and added three further tries in the 26th, 42nd and 71st minutes. Each time he scored, Lomu had time to look around to see what remained of the defence he had just decimated. Not much, just the shell of a broken rearguard. Eventually, when there was no way back for England – probably at 35–3 – even Lomu took his foot off the accelerator and the All Blacks coasted to a 45–29 victory, England salvaging a little pride in the final quarter with four tries; the same number scored in the opening 60 minutes by Lomu.

The Times reported that 'at the Sport Cafe in central London, where 800 fans gathered to urge on England, there was a palpable shock at the scale of New Zealand's superiority'. Lomu was to dominate the headlines for the next few days and become an international sensation. His triumph would give great satisfaction to Laurie Mains who always believed Lomu had the potential to become the star of the tournament, even though his faith in the giant No. 11 had been tested to the limit, especially when Lomu's fitness seemed to be letting him down so badly. Mains also took great pleasure from the near-perfect implementation of the game plan, one which had brought about the total disintegration of England.

Little wonder Mains was close to tears as he hugged the massive frame of New Zealand's new rugby legend at the end of the Newlands epic. In the space of four months the All Black coach had seen Lomu transformed from broken and despondent victim of Taupo's brutal regime, just a young kid who couldn't quite live up to the expectations of a hungry rugby nation, to awesome superstar of the greatest rugby show on earth. Even more remarkable, though, was the metamorphosis of character from self-destructive and self-defeating to self-disciplined and self-assured. As Lomu stood tall, elevated to the gods by the rapturous applause of the Cape Town crowd, it was hard to imagine that seven years earlier this product of South Auckland's poorest area had seen his future staring back at him as he stood over the dead body of his uncle.

Whether Lomu remembered this or other moments of his troubled past as he left the Newlands arena on 18 June 1995 is anyone's guess. In truth he could remember very little of the game and appeared to the world to be in some kind of daze – 'Pinch me, somebody pinch me' – but the words were lost in the emotional haze of his ascent to superstardom. Much later he would reveal: 'I was in fairyland when I walked off. It must have been the moment, the occasion, because I was completely out of it. I knew the team had done well; I knew I'd played well. But everything else was a blur. It was as though I was dreaming.'

Will Carling's nightmare continued as he watched the imposing figure of Lomu leave the field, and it wasn't until afterwards, when the shock had worn off, that the England captain was able to compose himself enough to deliver an honest verdict. All credit to Carling, though. He was gracious in defeat, describing the All Blacks as 'fast, dynamic and direct' and declaring Lomu 'an amazing athlete with incredible power whom we tried to stop, but couldn't', although his initial statement that 'he's awesome: he's a freak', is the quote that will live in the minds of rugby fans for all time. Tony Underwood, who had dared question Lomu's ability, chose to say nothing. Lomu still has the cutting although, being the modest man he is, he chose not to accept a lucrative offer to do a television commercial, which was going to feature a clip of him scoring his first try. It would have meant endless replays of him trampling over Mike Catt and Lomu admitted: 'It would have made me look like I was cocky and gloating. That's not what I am about. That's not Jonah Lomu. It was bad enough for Mike Catt that it was splashed all around the world. It didn't need me to push it any further. I don't believe in hurting other people's feelings to advance myself.'

And so it was back to Johannesburg where the greatest prize rugby has to offer beckoned Lomu and the rest of the All Blacks. South Africa had beaten France to take their place in the 1995 World Cup final and the whole world held its breath in anticipation of a match of epic proportions. In the meantime, though, Lomu had two promises to keep; to fly his mother and father out for the final and take Tanya Rutter out for dinner. It would be the last meal Lomu would enjoy for a long time.

11 GUTTED

Things sweet to taste prove in digestion sour.

– William Shakespeare, *Richard II*

It was soon after their arrival at the Holiday Inn in Pretoria, seven days before the final of the 1995 World Cup, that Jonah Lomu began to sense that fate may be turning against the All Blacks. It wasn't an obvious change of fortune or a rapid draining of luck but it was noticeable nevertheless, especially after the way things had gone for them since the start of the tournament. There was definitely something else in the air now; an ominous feeling of heaviness, like the thickening of the atmosphere before a storm. Only it wasn't a natural phenomenon, more of a sixth sense: an uneasy feeling. 'You couldn't quite put your finger on what it was,' he recalled. 'It was a strange sensation, like things were beginning to go against us, although on the outside everything appeared fine.'

Little things. It was the relatively insignificant happenings that began to undermine, only slightly at first, the prevailing mood of confidence at the Holiday Inn in Pretoria. Had Lomu kept his Walkman on, pulsating to the sound of funk and rap the whole time, he would probably have missed the signs of discontent: the odd whisper that all was not well, the occasional negative vibe. But he couldn't help but notice what was going on around him – the anxious faces, tense meetings, fraught phone calls, and the coming and going of people trying to stop things falling apart.

Initially it was a couple of phone calls between coach Laurie Mains and All Black physiotherapist Dr Mike Bowen, and between Mains and Kevin Roberts, chief operating officer for team sponsors Steinlager, that suggested fate could be turning against them. First of all Bowen called Mains to inform him that the hotel manager was being obstructive and was blocking every move to get the team chef to Johannesburg, and then Mains received a call from Roberts warning him that league and American football scouts were in town and planning to approach Lomu. This worried Mains because the threat of food poisoning (not an uncommon problem for sporting teams staying in South Africa), and security to prevent the potential costly distraction of players before the final, were two of the main trouble spots identified during a staff meeting following their return to Pretoria. They were not scheduled to move into their Johannesburg hotel until the Monday before Saturday's final against South Africa.

The last thing the All Blacks needed before then were the added burdens of worrying about the threat of food poisoning in the absence of their own trusted chef, and Lomu being pestered about his future. After further unsuccessful moves – largely thanks to opposition from the hotel manager – to fly the All Black chef from Cape Town to Johannesburg, Mains moved on to Plan B, which was to organize an eating strategy with the hotel management. Nor was he about to compromise Lomu's situation. Special precautions were taken: the player was moved to room with veteran All Black Frank Bunce who could keep an eye on the 20-year-old, around-the-clock bodyguards were arranged and it was agreed with security guards that there would be no telephone calls or fax messages direct to Lomu.

All requests from the press for interviews would be directed to media liaison officer Ric Salizzo and approaches from league and American football scouts, or anyone else, would be referred to either Mains or team manager Colin Meads. But no sooner had the security screen been put in place around Lomu than Mains received a call from the executive director of the Washington Redskins football team. He had received a call from a Redskins fan who had watched, on television in the United States, the All Blacks' game against England. The fan assured the executive director that Lomu was the best athlete he had ever seen, and that the club should buy him. So he somehow managed to find out where the All Blacks were staying in South Africa and called Mains, demanding to fax the necessary details of a four-year deal worth more than $US10 million through to Lomu. Mains refused and at the same time as he was doing so, a hundred or so miles away in Johannesburg, an otherwise unknown African woman by the name of Susie was figuring out how best to sabotage the All Blacks' World Cup plans without landing herself in jail.

A few days after the All Blacks' moved back to Johannesburg, security relating to the protection of Lomu deteriorated to such an extent that New Zealand rugby's hottest property became accessible to virtually anyone with the guile to find his room number; phone calls, which were supposed to be intercepted, were being put through to Lomu and fax messages, which were supposed to be forwarded to either Mains or Meads, were being slipped under his door. While investigating the events of the week before the final, I received a call from one of the security guards on duty at the hotel where the All Blacks stayed during the build-up to the 24 June clash with South Africa. He asked for anonymity, which was granted, but his version of events can be taken seriously because later they were corroborated by Mains and Frank Bunce.

'People started getting through to Lomu,' the security guard said. 'Some of my colleagues who were under orders to protect the guy began to turn a blind eye. After all they didn't want New Zealand to beat South Africa. It was a bad situation though, because any nutter with something to prove could have got to the guy, and believe me there were plenty of people around at that time who would have been happy to see Lomu put out of the game.'

Bunce said: 'Yeah, it's true. Security stopped doing their job and all kinds of people were getting through to Jonah, women wanting to take him out, people inviting him to their sister's birthday, guys who wanted to buy him a beer, journalists – he was being treated like public property. I thought, "What the hell's going on here?" I mean, we didn't need that kind of disruption.'

The security guard added: 'One night we got word that someone was planning to set off a car alarm right outside the hotel where the All Blacks were sleeping. The plan was to disrupt their sleep as much as possible so they were tired on the day of the match. We were told to ignore it and also turn a blind eye to anything else that went on. It was a conspiracy against the All Blacks, I am sure of it.'

Exactly who was conspiring against Mains and his team is uncertain but the All Blacks' coach said: 'In the small hours of the morning a car alarm went off. At 30-minute intervals for the remainder of the night for about seven or eight minutes at a time. And from 4 a.m. to 7 a.m. on the morning of the match, drums were moved around outside the kitchen, causing a terrible din. I confronted security about it but they said there was nothing they could do!'

With all this going on, Mains barely noticed the media stepping up their interest in Lomu, until a few days before the final when Shell instructed Radio 5FM, a local Johannesburg radio station, to offer a 5,000 rand (just under £1,000), bounty to any South African player who successfully tackled Lomu in the World Cup final. Mains went berserk and Shell withdrew the offer but the damage had already been done. The pressure was getting to Lomu and the rest of the All Black squad, although, apart from the noisy distractions, the media hype, and the absence of their own chef, the build-up had, remarkably, gone satisfactorily – albeit that was before the fateful lunch. If Susie had done her job properly the All Blacks would soon fear for their lives.

The luncheon assortment, two days before the final, consisted of lamb cutlets, crumbed fish, breast of chicken and pasta, with two or three green vegetables, potatoes, pumpkin and a selection of salads. It was presented as a buffet in the players' separate dining area. Tea and coffee were served from containers, which were replenished before the late arrival of Sean Fitzpatrick, Zinzan and Robin Brooke. Significantly, none of these three players would suffer any illness.

Approaching five o'clock that afternoon, Meads phoned Mains to say that Andrew Mehrtens was feeling unwell. At

6.30 p.m. Jeff Wilson, Richard Loe and Lomu reported to physio Dr Mike Bowen that they too felt unwell. Bowen then did the rounds, and, 20 minutes later, confronted Mains with the catastrophic news: the majority of the players were showing signs of having acute food poisoning. Many of them were vomiting uncontrollably and had diarrhoea. By 7.30 p.m. Mains and Meads had joined them. Bowen stayed awake throughout the night and received a steady stream of patients who, far from focusing on the World Cup final, doubted they would still be alive in the morning. 'It was a long night,' Lomu said. 'I wasn't as bad as some of the other guys, just a nasty bout of diarrhoea, but it still knocked me off my feet. Some of the guys didn't stop throwing up for two days.'

There is no doubt at all that if the World Cup final had been scheduled for that Friday, it would have been impossible for the All Blacks to put 15 players on the field. Mains and Meads seriously considered asking to have the match postponed for 24 hours but, because of the worldwide television commitments, that would have been impossible. In any case, the World Cup committee would probably have awarded the game to South Africa by default.

At the team meeting late on Friday afternoon, Mains assessed the damage. Some players were too sick to attend but the majority were slowly improving. Lomu even felt well enough to visit his parents who had been flown to Johannesburg to attend the final. By Saturday morning most of the Test squad felt well enough to play – in fact, all of them would take their place in the starting line-up. Most were clearly drained but some, including Lomu, appeared to have made almost a full recovery.

So Ellis Park, Johannesburg, the focal point of the sporting world on Saturday, 24 June 1995, began to echo with the sound of incoming fans and buzz with the prospect of hosting a multi-billion live television audience, while Jonah Lomu prayed. He asked God to help him and his team-mates play to the best of their ability, he prayed for strength to help them bounce back from the food poisoning, and for safety for all of the players involved. He also asked for a bit of luck, because right now the All Blacks needed all the help they could get.

Poisoning, as Susie was told by the people who allegedly paid her to spike the tea and coffee, leaves you weak, lacking drive. The urgency and aggression that had set the All Blacks apart from every other team at the World Cup were now missing. Most of their players were a metre or two slower than they had been; slower to breakdowns, producing slower ruck ball, and less accurate with their passing. And as the match progressed it became obvious to everyone watching that the All Blacks were not the same team that had torn apart Ireland, Wales, Scotland, and England. Somewhere in Johannesburg, probably in a run-down house in the poor outskirts of the city, a woman sat in a chair and realized what she had done. It was too late to say she was sorry, though, and as she listened to the radio she wondered if she could ever forgive herself for unfairly changing the course of sporting history.

Back at Ellis Park, Mains' courageous players hung on. After 80 minutes of regulation time New Zealand and South Africa were locked together at 9–9. Twenty minutes of extra time was ordered, but the All Black coach was not confident as he joined his weary players in the middle. He knew they couldn't take much more, and the sight of the ghost-like faces staring back at him almost reduced him to tears. It was unfair, so damned unfair. In the end, with the All Blacks close to exhaustion, their bodies debilitated by poison, Joel Stransky secured South Africa's victory with a dropped goal.

Lomu was shattered at the final whistle, perhaps more than most because had it not been for a controversial refereeing decision he could have won the game for the All Blacks. He said: 'My biggest nightmare was that pass from Walter Little. The referee ruled it forward, even though he was 20 metres behind play. It was not a forward pass – the TV replays showed that. The worst part of it all was there was no one in front of me, clear to the goal-line. It would have been a long run, but the adrenaline would have got me there.'

Most of the All Black players involved in the ill-fated final don't talk about it. Lomu himself would rather forget about it, although he says: 'Under the circumstances we didn't let anyone down. So many of us were exhausted from food poisoning, we expected to get thrashed. For me personally, it was a good World Cup, although I'd have swapped all of those tries for a winner's medal.'

A few days after the final Lindsay Singleton, managing director of Harvard Sports Marketing, picked up Gavin Laing, national sales manager for the Holiday Inn chain, from the All Blacks' hotel at Sandton, Johannesburg. As they headed to a meeting in Laing's car, Laing disclosed that he had just attended a staff meeting which had been called to investigate the apparent food poisoning of the All Blacks the previous Thursday.

Laing told Singleton that a black woman, working in the kitchen, had admitted she had put a 'substance' in the tea and coffee which was served in the All Blacks' dining room. He said the woman had confessed she was paid to do it, and, as a result of her actions, she had been dismissed by the hotel.

After this information was passed on to Laurie Mains, he engaged a private investigator in Johannesburg who was able to corroborate the story, although subsequent inquiries were thwarted by, what can only be described, as a cover-up. Mains said: 'The private investigator established that the woman, with a name sounding something like Susie, had been sacked because of her actions.'

These events tie in with Mains' original theory that it was most likely the tea and coffee that had done the damage. The Holiday Inn security guard I spoke to also corroborated the 'Susie-theory,' claiming: 'One of the guys in catering at the hotel in Sandton said he'd overheard a conversation between a delivery driver and one of the kitchen workers about a plan to put something in the tea and coffee. But I thought it was some kind of joke, until the All Blacks were poisoned.'

The three players who arrived late at lunch, Sean Fitzpatrick, Zinzan and Robin Brooke, were the only players who did not suffer food poisoning symptoms. They had enjoyed fresh brews of tea and coffee.

Several weeks after the World Cup final, the Holiday Inn manager sent a report to the All Blacks' media liaison officer Ric Salizzo saying that bottles of Periperi sauce – a hot Tabasco-like product – had been found in the players' rooms and sent for analysis. It had been established, he said, that the sauce contained high levels of bacteria and thus proved that this was the cause of the All Blacks' illness.

This was to become the official line, although Lomu established the absurdity of that claim when he later revealed: 'We got our Periperi sauce, as a souvenir, when we dined at a Portuguese restaurant on the Monday evening, three days after we had been laid low with food poisoning.'

For Lomu the whole episode should be laid to rest. 'It's history – over!' he said, 'there's no point in dragging it up. That's life, but I wouldn't want to go through anything like it again.'

Still under sieige from the media, rugby league scouts, and American football clubs for his awesome performance in the games against Ireland, Wales, Scotland, and England, Lomu couldn't wait to escape, although with a certain Tanya Rutter occupying his thoughts, New Zealand seemed an awfully long way to go.

12 UNTIL THE DUST SETTLES

Just keep quiet, boy, and play rugby.

Hepi Lomu

The poisoning was never mentioned at the official World Cup dinner but Lomu didn't want to talk about it anyway, not even with the new love of his life Tanya Rutter. What he did share with her was the agony of the defeat by South Africa, and how Walter Little's pass was legal and should have resulted in him scoring a try, probably the winning try. Lomu was angry about the decision and he told Tanya that he felt like punching the dressing room door off its hinges after the final. The injustice of the food poisoning and the refereeing decision was almost too much to bear, and Lomu felt like crying on Tanya Rutter's shoulder, although he didn't. Instead he had tears in his eyes when he met his mother Hepi and father Semisi after the final. He had wanted to win for them, as much as anyone else, and he had wanted to make Tanya the proudest woman in Johannesburg by signing her initials in the air again, even though the young South African student was torn between supporting her fellow-countrymen and urging

---

on the man she was falling in love with. It was a tough choice. In the end she almost got the perfect match, with the scores locked at 9–9. But there was always going to be only one winner, and she could see by the look in Jonah's eyes that it should have been New Zealand.

That didn't make defeat taste any sweeter, and Tanya did her best to try and lift Lomu's spirit by chatting about their future. Right now, as they gazed lovingly into each other's eyes, they could sense something good was happening. Lomu thought, 'If she makes me feel this good now, after everything that has happened this week, I never want to leave her.' The beginning of this love affair was the perfect tonic for the young New Zealand-Tongan who, after going through hell to make the All Black squad, had his heart set on a World Cup winner's medal. That the team had come so close, and ultimately against all the odds, tortured Lomu, but still he resisted the urge to drown his sorrows. On Sunday, save for the few individuals, including Lomu, who were teetotallers, Laurie Mains and his players drank themselves into oblivion, and who could blame them.

The acute sense of disappointment didn't ease over the next 72 hours before the All Blacks finally flew back into Auckland. The mood of the entire team was one of absolute dereliction: they had failed in achieving their ultimate goal, even though the rest of the world didn't see it that way. The civic reception held outside the Auckland town hall in Aotea Square on their return to New Zealand confirmed this. The weather was lousy but the turnout was huge and it was reassuring for Mains and his players to realize finally that the rugby people of New Zealand thought the All Blacks were heroes, not losers. They were praised for lifting the game to new heights, although Lomu admits: 'Most of us wanted to slip back into the country un-noticed. We didn't want a fuss because we had failed to win the World Cup. We appreciated the support of the people but it didn't make it any easier. It didn't ease the pain.'

It wasn't all doom and gloom for Lomu, however, because if the World Cup had done nothing else, at least it had firmly established him as a force to be reckoned with in world rugby, and an expensive one at that. At this point in his life Lomu could easily have become a millionaire overnight. The rollercoaster had taken him from the high of his All Black trial in 1994 to the low of the disappointment of his first two Test matches, through the hell of the Taupo training camp and the confusion of the TV3 nightmare, and back up to the heights of World Cup rugby and his awesome display against England, before hurtling back down to earth in the wake of the devastating defeat against South Africa. Now the rollercoaster had levelled out again. Lomu had time to catch his breath and, to a certain degree, enjoy the ride and the view.

In terms of his immediate future, Lomu wasn't looking no further than the two Bledisloe Cup test matches against Australia in Auckland on 12 July and in Sydney a week later. In truth, Mains and his players had little time to dwell on the disappointment of South Africa. The Bledisloe Cup, which had changed hands three times in three years, was not in All Black hands and they wanted it back. Lomu was particularly looking forward to the match in Sydney, mainly because Tanya would be there and immediately afterwards they were scheduled to fly up to the north coast of Australia for a week's holiday. There, in the winter sunshine, the pair would make a big decision about their future. In the meantime, though,

Lomu had a big decision of his own to make; whether to pursue a career in union or explore the possibility of switching to league or even American football.

Representatives of the Washington Redskins and Dallas Cowboys had followed Lomu from Johannesburg to Auckland and were planning to watch him in action against Australia, but only if he showed some interest in what they had to offer. After the World Cup final Mains had informed Lomu about the Redskins offer, and he also told the player to expect a call from the Cowboys as well. Had Lomu not already decided against the idea of moving to the United States, the Bledisloe Cup matches would probably have taken place alongside an auction between Washington and Dallas for the services of the All Black winger. Lomu could have become a multi-millionaire overnight. British rugby league clubs Leeds and Wigan were also on Lomu's trail, but like the Americans they did not hold out much hope of signing him, especially after Lomu had gone on the record as saying, during an awards ceremony in Johannesburg a few days after the World Cup final, that he had no immediate intention of deserting rugby union. Asked if he would still be an All Black in four years' time he replied: 'I hope so. Money talks for some people but not me. Some people take the money but I don't think about that.'

It was a sincere response, although Lomu, who at that time was still working as a bank officer, later admitted that the thought of becoming a millionaire had caused him a few sleepless nights, especially after Leeds and Wigan improved their initial offers by several hundred thousand pounds. The Yorkshire and Lancashire league clubs were prepared to offer him long-term contracts in excess of £1.5 million each. Lomu was also being pursued by Kerry Packer for his projected rugby union circus in which the leading players of the 1995 World Cup would receive around £200,000 each. At the same time Rupert Murdoch was locked in negotiations with the rugby unions of Australia, New Zealand, and South Africa over a $500 million ten-year television deal to embrace annual Tri-Nations Test matches, and the Super 10 was becoming the Rugby Super 12, involving the best provincial teams from those three nations.

As the All Blacks prepared to meet Australia in Auckland for the first Bledisloe Cup Test match, and Lomu was making a final decision about his future, Richie Guy, chairman of the NZRFU, issued a warning that any player known to be involved in Packer's proposed World Rugby Championship would be dropped from the national team and suspended from all rugby. The NZRFU had already agreed, in principle, a £340 million deal, alongside the Australian Unions, to play in the new international and provincial series backed by Packer's media rival Murdoch. In addition, the word on the Auckland grapevine hinted that any All Black player talking to British league clubs would be overlooked for the Bledisloe Cup matches. Even had Lomu not virtually made up his mind to remain an All Black, the decision had been taken out of his hands. There was no way he was going to provoke the wrath of the NZRFU and end up leaving New Zealand under a cloud. Weeks earlier he had confided in his mother Hepi saying: 'If I leave I want people to accept and be happy with my decision, else I couldn't live with it.' That was an impossible dream and even if Hepi had given the move her blessing, which would never have happened, Lomu wasn't completely happy with the idea of leaving his home. When all the cards were on the table the only sensible hand left for Lomu to play was to stick with what he'd already got. In the end the NZRFU came up with an attractive long-term package designed to keep their hottest property content and allegedly worth in excess of $NZ 2 million a year, although the exact figure has never been confirmed.

In hindsight it was the best possible move for Lomu who now admits: 'I wouldn't have been happy playing league in England, and, although I could have turned my hand to American football, I definitely would not have been happy in the United States. I got some silly offers to switch codes after the World Cup. Some of the offers were huge, out of this world. I find it funny when people say, "Look at Jonah, he's filthy rich now." Not true. If I'd wanted to be filthy rich I wouldn't have stayed with rugby. That's what people don't know. They don't understand. They think I got a bigger offer from rugby union. I didn't. I wanted to play rugby union. I enjoyed the game; I wanted the jersey. Bad. The money? All I wanted was to be financially secure. Stay in New Zealand. Live comfortably. Nothing over the top. The NZRFU came up with a reasonable offer and I didn't think twice about taking it.'

Lomu didn't think twice about accepting the gauntlet thrown down by Laurie Mains either. The All Black coach, concerned that Lomu might be unsettled by the intense media interest, unaffected by his decision to remain in New Zealand, set about focusing the player's mind on the immediate challenges that lay ahead. 'Let your rugby do the talking,' he said. 'You've shown the world what you are capable of, now show them again.'

The All Black team had won nothing so far in 1995. They'd been to the World Cup and come second; played the best rugby but come home empty-handed. What made it worse was that the international media were only interested in Lomu, and the brilliant performance of Mains' team in South Africa was no longer an issue. The Springboks were the new world champions and New Zealand were, for the moment, history. That hurt Mains, because in his heart he knew that the best team did not win the World Cup; instead the best team had been the victim of an outrageous injustice and cheated of their rightful inheritance, and apart from the support of the New Zealand people and a small section of the media the All Black team had been abandoned to their fate.

'It was a bad time for the All Black team,' Lomu said. 'We knew we were better than second best, but that's how the rest of the world saw us. The team that South Africa beat in the final. Laurie Mains didn't want us to accept that, he demanded that we end 1995 on a high note, he challenged each one of us to get over the disappointment. Our pride was still intact but we still needed to win something. We needed the tonic of success.'

Mains added: 'We wanted, as a team, to show we hadn't left our achievements, or our playing style, at the World Cup. We wanted to demonstrate that the dynamic new game we had developed was now a permanent part of All Black rugby.'

So Lomu and the rest of the All Black team made the Bledisloe Cup their focus, as well as the Test matches against Italy and France which would follow two months later in late October and early November. In total New Zealand had five Tests – including a double-header against the French – to get South Africa out of their system. 'Let's win them all,' Mains declared, and they very nearly did, with Lomu immediately paying back a substantial slice of the money invested in him by the NZRFU.

Initially, as the Bledisloe Cup matches loomed, Mains was alarmed to find that Lomu hadn't played, and indeed had basically done nothing, since the World Cup. He wasn't injured but he was mentally tired and emotionally drained. South Africa had been an intense experience, especially the food poisoning incident and the subsequent agony of the extra-time defeat by the Springboks in the final. Worse still for Mains, a number of players had returned from South Africa with injuries that would keep them out of rugby in the three weeks through to the first Bledisloe Cup match against Australia at Auckland's Eden Park, and the World Rugby Championship developments were having an unsettling effect on the team.

The All Blacks emerged successful at Eden Park but only after a hard-fought battle against an Australian team determined to salvage its reputation after losing to England in the quarter-finals of the World Cup. The All Blacks trailed 10–9 at half-time and were still behind 16–15 with nine minutes to play. In an extraordinary finish, Andrew Mehrtens, whose usually brilliant precision kicking had been so cruelly affected by food poisoning during the World Cup final, converted five penalty goals and two dropped goals to put the All Blacks ahead 21–16 with less than two minutes remaining. Time was as good as up before New Zealand managed a try; a spectacular 80-metre move started by Frank Bunce and finished by Lomu. It was the eighth Test match try of his career and gave the All Black team a 28–16 victory. Now all they had to do was to win in Sydney to regain the Bledisloe Cup.

It would be an historic game for several reasons. Firstly, it would be the last time Mike Brewer and Graham Bachop would represent New Zealand, because Bachop, a veteran halfback of rare ability, was heading back to Japan and Brewer, who had one of his best ever games as blindside flanker during the World Cup semi-final against England, was retiring. Secondly, it was the 100th Test between New Zealand and Australia, and thirdly, with the developments on the WRC front reaching an inevitable conclusion, it would be the last amateur Test between the two countries. It was also Lomu's Bledisloe Cup debut.

On the eve of the Sydney Test, Bob Dwyer, the Australian coach, was quoted in the New Zealand press as saying 'I don't think there has been anything like him', referring to Lomu. Mains was thinking the same thing, only not about the player's rugby ability. The All Black coach was finding it difficult to tolerate Lomu's laid-back attitude, especially his arrival at team meetings throughout the World Cup tournament wearing ear phones. Image is a big thing for Lomu; the clothes, the hair, the music. He was brought up with rap and reggae and plays it so loud that he once blew the back wind-screen out of his car. He loves to experiment with his look. He had hair extensions once and got the number 11 shaved in his eyebrow just before the World Cup. 'I'll try anything once,' he said. 'If I'm in the mood, watch out.'

He was definitely 'in the mood' before the Sydney Test on 19 July 1995; so laid-back he sauntered into the team room around 12.45 p.m. on the Saturday, not only with his Walkman on, but wearing a flash pair of sunglasses. Mains couldn't believe it. The All Black team was poised to take on Australia in a match of vital importance and Lomu, arguably their most dangerous asset, was acting like he didn't care. This nonchalance was becoming a familiar trademark and many of the All Black players were unhappy with the attitude of a team-mate who appeared to be showing all the signs of

someone who had let fame and fortune go to his head. Mains'
natural instinct was to confront Lomu but, being the shrewd
coach and man-manager he is, he thought better of it, largely
because Lomu, who hadn't played that well in the first
Bledisloe Cup match in Auckland, had had a tough build-up
during the week and had been totally committed in training.
So the All Black coach carried on with his team talk as if
nothing was different. Lomu just sat there with his Walkman
and shades on, but all the time he was psyching himself up.
What Mains and the rest of the All Blacks didn't know was
that their hottest property was pumping himself up for
another awesome display.

Within two minutes Lomu had signalled his intent to run
the show. Mehrtens threw a skip pass and Lomu suddenly had
the ball with 15 metres to spare. In that situation he is lethal.
With one shrug of his powerful shoulders he bumped off his
marker, sucked in and spat out two more and hurtled down
the left touchline. He was at last brought to ground 10 metres
from the Australian line, but not before he got a pass to Bunce
for the try. The All Blacks went on to score five tries in the
game, three of which Lomu set up, and one of which he
scored. He was simply unstoppable and was named man of the
match as Mains' team registered their second successive win
over Australia, 34–23, to win the Bledisloe Cup.

Two highly respectable rugby writers, Sir T. P. McLean and
Greg Dowden, summed it up perfectly. 'Let's be fair to the boy,'
said veteran New Zealand journalist McLean. 'Let's not go
overboard and say the game has never produced his equal.
Let's, rather, get down on our hands and knees to thank heaven
for sending us, at this hour, so extraordinary a match-winner.'
Dowden, the *Sydney Sun-Herald* journalist, wrote: 'Australia

became the latest victim of the Jonah Lomu factor when the greatest attacking force in international rugby swept the Wallabies aside ... he is the rugby phenomenon of the '90s.'

For Lomu, there was the immense personal satisfaction of almost single-handedly winning back the Bledisloe Cup and the moment got to him. As most of the players were changing after their showers, Lomu removed from his bag a CD player, placed it on top of the lockers, turned the volume to maximum, filling the room with heavy reggae music, and proceeded to dance. He roared with laughter and danced and danced until he could dance no more. Significantly, Lomu had found himself and had the confidence to express himself, and soon he had many of his fellow All Blacks dancing too. It was the best victory party Mains had ever seen.

It was certainly a good time for Lomu, although there was a cloud on the horizon, the darkening of his now bright immortality, which would take him completely by surprise and almost end his career. But for now he could enjoy life, and feel content with his place in the world. He was a star, shining out as the brightest prospect in the game, and the world was his. In Cape Town, mid-September 1995, South African rugby fans, of all people, rated Lomu a ten times better player than Will Carling, of all players. The All Black rugby jersey which Lomu wore for the World Cup final, raised 8,000 rand ($2,191), while Carling's rugby boots, also used during the tournament, only went for 700 rand ($191). The auction raised a total of 100,000 rand (US $27,000) for paralysed Ivory Coast right wing Max Brito, injured during the World Cup. Several weeks later Lomu won the awards for New Zealand player of the year and sevens player of the year.

It was also a good month for Mains, who finally got what he wanted for his All Blacks; an unprecedented deal with the WRC and NZRFU that meant none of his players would go to league because they would be earning so much in union. The game went professional and, by contract, the players were together for three years; New Zealand rugby was destined to become pre-eminent because of the ten-year Murdoch deal; and the elite of rugby would compete with each other every week thanks to the Super 12 and Tri-Nations competitions.

The All Black team, however, had one final challenge ahead of them before the end of 1995, a tour of Italy and France that would include three Test matches and provide Lomu with a chance to erase the painful memory of his first Tests against the French in the New Zealand winter of 1994. The tour would also hand Lomu his European debut, 16 months after he became the youngest ever All Black. Going to France would also raise a question of personal conscience for Lomu. He was opposed to France's nuclear testing, although he refused to voice his criticism publicly as other players, including Sean Fitzpatrick and Zinzan Brooke, eventually did at the first All Black news conference of the tour.

Lomu's European debut in a one-off Test against Italy in Bologna on 28 October 1995, was overshadowed by a serious injury to his friend and team-mate Andrew Mehrtens, who ruptured his cruciate knee ligaments in a warm-up against Italy A at Catania. Lomu was deeply upset by Mehrtens' plight but it didn't stop him from marking his European debut with two spectacular tries as the All Blacks overwhelmed Italy 70–6. After losing control when tempers flared in a first-half ruck, Lomu gathered his composure to make two devastating solo runs, scoring his first try from the halfway line while contemptuously brushing off three would-be tacklers and running the ball the full length of the field for his second. It prompted Italian coach Georges Coste to remark: 'He is like a freight train. He has been destroying players from England to Italy.'

Coste also described the All Blacks as being 'like a team from another planet', after they swept away his side for an unstoppable victory. With Lomu sporting a fashionable goatee beard and pumped full of heavy rap and reggae, the All Black team cruised through their provincial matches in the build-up to the first Test against the French in Toulouse. Five outings, of which two were in Italy, had netted them 28 tries. The one difficulty Lomu was having was picking up the lingo. The only words of French he knew were 'bonjour' and 'merci' and as a result he spent a lot of time on the telephone talking with his parents and girlfriend Tanya Rutter. Hepi Lomu's best advice was: 'Just keep quiet, boy, and play rugby.'

Gale force south-easterlies, whipping in a frenzy from the Mediterranean, and heavy rain made it virtually impossible for anyone to play rugby, let alone Lomu, when the All Black team met the French for the first of two Test matches in mid-November 1995. The Toulouse game on Sunday, 11 November ended in disaster. Several times they were blatantly offside by metres but got away with it, scoring three tries when each time the All Blacks should have been awarded a penalty, and also playing offside around the scrum which allowed them to charge down All Black kicks.

The 22–15 victory to France not only completed a hat-trick for them against New Zealand but also ended an impressive All Black record. Before Toulouse, they had scored 13 wins and suffered only one setback, the extra-time defeat against South Africa in the World Cup final.

The rain-lashed first French Test left Lomu feeling drained. He trudged off the pitch at the end and later admitted: 'I was completely whacked and I had health problems – boils and some kind of minor blood disorder. I was tired coming into the Toulouse game. Right at the end of the Italy game, I remember yelling to Stu Forster to pass me the ball. The wing I was marking was caught in a maul. I got the pass, looked up and thought, "Oh, no, now I've got to run 90 metres for this try." I was knackered, I kept saying, "Why did I do that?"'

It was an ominous sign, but the full extent of Lomu's medical problems were as yet far from being diagnosed. The only thing on his mind as the All Blacks prepared for their final two games of the tour, against a French Selection XV in Nancy and the full French side in Paris, was going home and seeing his family, and of course Tanya Rutter, who was by this time considering emigrating to New Zealand. 'The first Test against France was a nightmare for me,' Lomu said. 'After 1994 I was thinking "Here we go again." The boys were really on edge after that loss. It had been a long season and we were homesick. We just wanted to drill the French, even up the series and get home.'

Since the infamous shock defeat at Penrith in 1992, the All Black team had not lost a midweek encounter, so it was a great relief when two tries each by Lomu and fullback Glen Osborne contributed to a 55–17 demolition of the French Selection in Nancy on 14 November 1995. Lomu was again man of the match, virtually smashing the local defence at will as Mains' team scored eight tries in a hopelessly one-sided game. But it was the perfect tonic to raise spirits before the 18 November Test against France at the Parc des Princes. The All Black team would need every ounce of mental strength to avenge the Toulouse defeat, and they would need Lomu firing on all cylinders.

He tried to rest as much as possible in the three days between Nancy and Paris but was less than 80 per cent fit when Laurie Mains' favourite referee, Australian Peter Marshall, got the final game of New Zealand's tour under way. It would prove to be an exhausting 80 minutes for Lomu but a glorious day for the All Black team, who produced a performance equal to their display against England in Cape Town to defeat the French 37–12. The home nation stitched Lomu up this way and that, but he still found the pace and power to plough straight through the middle of the French defence, with Alain Penaud and Philippe Benetton lying in his wake, to crown a brilliant victory with a try of earth-shaking force.

Three days later, desperately homesick and travel-weary, Lomu showed the generous side of his nature by appearing in a testimonial for former Wales captain Ieuan Evans at Llanelli. The fact that Lomu's manager Phil Kingsley-Jones hails from neighbouring Blaina, the old Gwent mining town, had something to do with the All Black winger's appearance on a cold November night, but Lomu wanted to help out and his presence guaranteed a capacity crowd of 13,000 and an estimated £70,000 for Evans. It was a touching gesture and so was his willingness to sign autographs for the hundreds of young Llanelli rugby fans who waited patiently for him afterwards.

Still, he couldn't wait to get back home. He had spent the best part of the year touring and now, especially with the added pull of his new relationship with Tanya Rutter, he just wanted to spend some quality time with the people who mattered most to him. Little did he know that he was heading for a major domestic crisis, one that would shake the very foundations of his relationship with his parents. As Lomu brought Christmas presents and called Tanya several times on his way home to Auckland, another cloud began to loom on the horizon. Marriage.

13 SWEETHEART, BROKEN HEART

O swear not by the moon, the inconstant
moon, that monthly changes in her
circled orb, lest that thy love prove
likewise variable.

William Shakespeare, *Romeo and Juliet*

Tuesday in March, autumn in New Zealand. Jonah Lomu faces his family as he has never done before. In the South Auckland home of his Tongan parents, Hepi and Semisi, the core of the Lomu family have gathered as if at a wake. Almost everyone who lives at Maitland Place, the mainly Tongan but also New Zealand Caucasian occupants of the dozen small wooden homes, know what is going on at number 8a. If they haven't heard it on the news or read it in the paper they have certainly heard it on the grapevine. Jonah has done something terrible, maybe even unforgiveable, and you can almost feel the weight of their heavy hearts as the realization of what has taken place 72 hours earlier, only a few miles down the road, begins to sink in.

Hepi's eyes are red and swollen after two days of non-stop tears while Semisi has a face like thunder – but he too feels like crying. At first they could not believe what Jonah has done, now they only struggle to understand why. There is no longer any doubt that he has done this terrible deed, this act of family betrayal, and it certainly cannot be undone. The only thing left for them to do is to confront their 20-year-old son and ask for a reason. They want the truth and they have to face it now, before the terrible situation causes a rift beyond repair.

This may be the moment when Jonah Lomu finally broke his mother's heart. In the past, especially during his self-confessed 'days when I was out of control', Jonah had caused Hepi Lomu times of great anxiety and upset. But he never intentionally hurt her or did anything so serious as to inflict emotional or mental wounds too severe to heal. He was a bad boy, some of the time, but had always, until this inconceivable moment of insensitivity, acknowledged his parents' important role in his life, their status as respected elders of a tight-knit community. Perhaps more importantly, they were the two people who had done most to nurture not only his talent but his appreciation and love of his heritage, of which he is immensely proud.

The fact that he had neglected to tell them about his marriage to 19-year-old South African Tanya Rutter or invite them to the wedding came as an even greater shock in the light of a newspaper interview with Jonah the previous month. In it he had talked passionately about his 'close relationship' with his parents, who he described as 'the most important people in my life'. No one doubted his sincerity, but the scene that greeted reporters and TV news crews as they arrived in Mangere two days after the wedding was one of sickening disbelief. Friends and neighbours of Hepi and Semisi Lomu wanted to confront Jonah themselves to vent their anger at what they saw as a blatant act of contempt. 'They'll never forgive him for this' and 'he may as well have spit on their graves', are examples of the kind of comments people in Mangere East were coming out with. Certainly, Lomu may as well have stolen the bloody crown jewels for the way he was condemned for his actions but, in truth, he had taken something much more valuable from Hepi and Semisi; their trust.

Over two years later when I visited them at their Mangere home to research this book the subject of the secret wedding remained partially taboo. They were not comfortable talking about it and the general consensus among neighbours was that the wounds had not yet completely healed. That is not surprising if you understand the high value placed on family unity within the Tongan community. The Tongan individual is defined by his family, and the family is defined by the individuals of the family. There is little that can be done in the Tongan community without the need for the involvement of the family, whether it be the complex task of rearing of a child or the maintenance of land holdings, a household, or planning a wedding.

Maybe, deep in his own altered psyche – changed by the overwhelming feeling of immortality real success and power creates – Jonah Lomu believed that his family would understand the need for secrecy. After all he was now an international sporting celebrity and the whole world, mesmerized by the awesomeness of his 1995 World Cup performance, were making demands on his personal life they had no right to. In effect he was running scared from the consequences of his own exceptional talent.

There was another reason for his controversial decision, which he later described as 'the biggest mistake of my life' – fear. Jonah was afraid his parents would prohibit the match. And they probably would have done, first because she is not a Tongan and, to a lesser degree, because the relationship was still in its infancy – not quite ten months old. Although Hepi, or Semesi for that matter, have never publicly admitted that they are opposed to the idea of a mixed marriage, it is common knowledge among the residents of the Tongan community in South Auckland that Hepi wanted Jonah to wed a Tongan girl. There are even rumours to suggest that she had a potential wife in mind, although it has to be said that Tanya has since been accepted as 'one of the family', to quote Semisi Lomu.

Back in the New Zealand autumn of 1996, though, Jonah's fear of his parents' disapproval reduced him to tears on more than one occasion during that emotionally charged week. The whole of Auckland and most of the rest of the country sat open-mouthed, mainly loving every minute of it, as the drama unfolded with all the intrigue and sensationalism of a soap opera. Jonah's love affair with Tanya, the daughter of a semi-retired printer from a small South African town, was no secret. But although the romance, which had begun during the World Cup in Johannesburg, was unabashed in its carefree passion, the prospect of marriage was not even on the agenda of public speculation let alone family discussion, even when Miss Rutter moved to New Zealand shortly before Christmas 1995. Before that, in the six months between the World Cup and his future wife's emigration, Jonah Lomu had returned three times to South Africa, presumably to further consummate the relationship that in his own words 'means more to me than rugby'. Suddenly an unknown, but very attractive, teenage social science student had taken priority in the life of potentially one of the biggest attractions in modern sport. In Lomu's lovestruck eyes Tanya Rutter is more important than the All Blacks and God, and in that order.

Interviewed on the *Holmes Show*, one of New Zealand's most popular chat shows, on the night of the parentless wedding – not even Tanya's mother and father were let in on the secret – Jonah Lomu broke down in tears as he attempted to explain why he had snubbed Hepi and Semisi. He said not having his mother with him on his wedding day 'was the hardest thing', but insisted that he had a very good reason for marrying his sweetheart without notifying them: 'I was scared they wouldn't let me do it,' he said as genuine tears of relief and sorrow continued to fall in front of a TV audience of around half a million people. Relief because he was glad he had gone through with it and could now tell the whole world; sorrow because he knew what it had done to his parents, especially his mother Hepi, who felt her heart might break completely in two as she read the news for the first time in a newspaper, two days after the wedding.

Why Jonah failed to break the news to her before the media did remains one of life's great mysteries. She was only a phone call away, and a 20-minute drive after the ceremony would have softened the blow, but she and her husband Semisi never received a call from their son on that Sunday evening. That is something Jonah Lomu has to live with for the rest of his life, even though he is now forgiven. 'It took us a while to come to terms with what happened,' she said, three years later, 'but we did and now we are very happy for them.'

Not so at the time, when the newborn star of world rugby introduced his new wife to New Zealand before Tanya had paid her first visit to 8a Maitland Place as Mrs Jonah Lomu. Hepi was less forgiving then. In fact she was more angry than she had been in her whole life and the excuses, bleated out in tearful self-defence by her son, were meaningless. He had told everyone the same thing, reinforcing it time and time again as if to convince himself that what he was saying contained some truth, if only enough to take some of the sting out of the situation. 'I wanted to tell my parents myself immediately afterwards,' he said, 'but everybody seems to have beaten me to it. It wasn't the way I expected it to happen.'

What Lomu lacked in sensitivity he made up for in naivety. Did he think it was possible to marry in secret and keep the news from Hepi and Semisi until he got around to telling them, when a dozen reporters and at least one TV crew were hanging around, two streets away from where the ceremony took place? Incredibly yes, even though the person entrusted to plan and carry off without major incident the social event of the decade was at that time a bigger sports celebrity than the man who was attempting to marry in secret! The marriage took place on the banks of Manukau Harbour in Auckland in a civil ceremony organized by fellow All Black, Michael Jones, who was best man. It was written in the stars in indelible neon lights that the fastest All Black alive would not beat the press to his mother's door.

As if to seal his own fate, Lomu agreed to appear with his new bride on New Zealand television before he was due to see his parents in Mangere East. The excited media couldn't wait to get there. The newspaper and television-populated convoy of cars and vans must have triggered speed guns all the way through the city and out over the Mangere Bridge in their haste for an exclusive reaction. One particular tabloid journalist, armed with a quote from Rose Franklin, who conducted the service, came close to provoking the full wrath of Semisi Lomu after refusing to move from the front porch of the house at Maitland Place. The Lomus, however, handled the situation with great composure and dignity even though they were visibly embarrassed and hurt.

Franklin, describing the clandestine ceremony, said: 'It was magical. The sun was starting to set. There was a marvellous big moon. Just as I introduced them as Mr and Mrs Lomu, the sun set. It was terrific.' Hepi was unimpressed. 'How come other people know first and then I know later from someone else? I'm not sure I can ever make it up with him,' she said. 'I feel so confused about it and disappointed a lot.' Semisi Lomu refused to believe that his son had married. 'He is a good boy,' he said. 'He would never go and get married without telling his mother or discussing it with me.'

Tanya Rutter's parents, however, were more than happy about the news even though they also suffered the indignity of being kept in the dark They instantly attempted to cash in on their new-found celebrity. 'I've already been offered five thousand bucks (£1,000) for the whole story,' said her father Alan from the family's modest bungalow in Kimberley. 'If you want the whole story let's see what you can come up with.' Several weeks later, or so the story goes, a New Zealand newspaper offered Alan Rutter $50,000. But that is only a fraction of the amount the Lomu family received from a glossy society magazine for exclusive rights to cover the second wedding, which took place in South Africa. According to Jonah and Tanya, it was planned all along, although it is said with some justification that the decision to stage an 'official' ceremony was made after the secret wedding in South Auckland and not before. It was a form of emotional payback, a big sorry from Jonah to his mother who allegedly gave her son an ultimatum on that Tuesday evening in Mangere – 'Make amends or I'll never forgive you.'

If this is true then Jonah more than made up for the terrible mistake he made when he and Tanya decided to wed in secret, although perhaps the highly impressive and expensive ceremony in Tanya Rutter's home town of Kimberley achieved nothing more than to restore a little dignity to Hepi and Semisi Lomu. At least Hepi can now look her friends and relatives in the eye and say 'It was a beautiful wedding', and she has the photographs to prove it. But for Jonah, the pressure of worldwide media attention continued to increase, to the extent that at one stage he had second thoughts about the big wedding in South Africa.

Before the secret ceremony on the banks of Manukau Harbour, Lomu had admitted to Michael Jones – a born-again Christian and a steadying influence on Jonah during the early days of his All Black career – and his Wales-based manager Phil Kingsley-Jones, that the often claustrophobic atmosphere of mega-stardom had started to affect his game, although several weeks later he went to great lengths to deny suggestions by Kingsley-Jones that he was considering leaving rugby. 'It was a thought, that's all,' he insisted. 'I love rugby.' Former All Black coach Laurie Mains, who offered Lomu a shoulder to lean on during the times when he doubted he could cope with the pressure, said: 'Being in the public eye has put a tremendous pressure on a young man who, when he came into rugby at this level, hadn't been trained on how to deal with it.'

But at least now he had the support of his beautiful young wife, who gave up her studies in social work to be with him, and as a friend in Bloemfontein, South Africa pointed out: 'They are obviously deeply in love. It came as no surprise to us that they are married, although it has clearly taken some people by surprise, and not just Jonah's parents.'

It was a loaded remark aimed at the army of female admirers, mainly young and beautiful and in New Zealand, who were also left broken-hearted when Jonah and Tanya became husband and wife. As the setting sun disappeared beneath the horizon where the Manukau sky meets the Tasman Sea on the evening of Sunday 17 March 1996, so did the dreams of every girl and woman who wanted to marry the tall, dark and handsome Islander. Still, they could hope, and this is something Tanya Lomu would have to live with as long as her husband remained an object of desire.

Lomu's pulling power is even recognized by the Maori opera singer Dame Kiri Te Kanawa. The attractive 54-year-old New Zealander, like Lomu a legend in her own lifetime, is qualified to comment on the 'it' factor as she herself has been, and still is, an object of desire for men, and women, the world over. Cinema audiences will remember Kiri as the ravishingly beautiful Donna Elvira in Joseph Losey's *Don Giovanni*. England fell in love with her in 1971 following her sensational portrayal of the Countess in Mozart's *The Marriage of Figaro* at Covent Garden, and America did the same three years later during Kiri's celebrated and deeply sensual debut at the New York Met as Desdemona in Verdi's *Otello*. In 1990 at her outdoor concert in Auckland, which attracted 140,000 people – the largest crowd ever to hear a solo artist – they sold out of roses, such was the romantic appeal of her presence, and nine years earlier, when she sang at the wedding of Prince Charles and Lady Diana Spencer, Kiri was overwhelmed with male admirers. Ironically, her own wedding in 1967 dominated the news like no other nuptials until Jonah wed Tanya.

At the 1995 World Cup in South Africa, nine months before Lomu's Auckland wedding, Dame Kiri described Jonah as 'gorgeous', and added that 'every New Zealand girl wants to marry him'. An ardent supporter of the All Blacks, Kiri would have been tempted to do so herself had she been available and, with the utmost respect, a few years younger. 'He is a very attractive man,' she added, 'and he is going to be in demand until he marries and even then I doubt they'll leave him alone.'

Kiri was right. A month after he wed Tanya, Jonah was fighting them off during a trip to his favourite city Hong Kong, where it became perfectly clear that marriage is no obstacle to fan lust. Tanya Rutter or no Tanya Rutter the ladies will continue to chase after rugby's 'Incredible Hunk' – to borrow a term from the Hong Kong press. When he was in Hong Kong for the 1996 Sevens tournament, which the All Blacks won, Lomu caused a near riot when he turned up for an auto-graph-signing session at a sports store. Screaming girls and panting women trampled over one another in a desperate attempt to push their way to the front of what can only be described as a unusually inviting scrum outside the shop. 'I love him to death,' gushed one female fan. 'Jonah, kiss me,' begged another, before the police arrived to restore law and order and rescue Jonah from a fate many would gladly wish upon themselves.

Less than two months later the sight of Lomu, or more precisely his buttocks, caused another near riot at Auckland's Eden Park rugby ground. After watching him suffer the not uncommon indignity of having his shorts split, while helping the Auckland Super 12 team to defeat Natal, a group of around a dozen female followers – maybe they could be called groupies – went wild and had to be restrained by stewards. Lomu was equipped with a new pair of shorts, and the remnants of the old were left in the mud as the game ended. Several of the girl fans tried to get their hands on the split shorts but they were prevented from going on to the field of play. In the end former All Black, MP, and radio commentator Grahame Thorne somehow managed to give ground security the slip to get his hands on the shorts, which he thought would make an ideal souvenir to add to his collection of rugby memorabilia.

He tucked them under his arm, and was leaving the field when a hand on his shoulder stopped him dead in his tracks. It was the New Zealand Prime Minister wanting to have a friendly word, unaware of Thorne's ill-gotten prize. Thorne would have got away with it had he not boasted to a member of the press that he had Lomu's ripped pants in his possession. The word quickly spread, unfortunately for the rugby player-turned-politician straight to a senior official of the Auckland Rugby Union who immediately laid claim to the shorts, before asking Lomu what he wanted to do with them. Lomu didn't want Thorne to have them so he told the ARU to auction them for charity. It wasn't going to be that simple though. Thorne refused to part with them and after several days of 'yes he should, no I won't', he finally surrendered the dirty and torn but much sought-after pants live on the *Holmes Show*. He was promised an alternative souvenir from Jonah to compensate for his loss. Whether he ever received one remains unclear but the shorts raised $1,000 for charity, and not surprisingly the highest bidder was female.

Tanya Rutter always knew that this kind of thing came with the territory. She'd seen it all before during their short but intense courtship: girls throwing themselves at Jonah, desperate for only a moment of his attention, eye contact, a smile, absolutely anything substantial enough to stand the test of time as a cherished memory of 'the day I met Jonah'. It did not matter if he didn't say a word, a silent acknowledgement would do and sometimes even less. Just to see him, be close to him, shout his name. There are times when it gets out of hand and sometimes it's not just the female fans who run wild. Lomu revealed: 'I've been in situations where people have actually thrown their kids at me just to try and get my autograph. It's frightening stuff. I've had my shirt literally torn off my back, I've been grabbed around the neck by over-excited women, shoved and pushed around despite my size, and attacked.'

That happened at a provincial match in August 1995 when he was punched and jostled by spectators. Lomu's club side Counties Manukau had just beaten Canterbury 41–39 at Pukekohe when a punch was thrown at Lomu by a spectator as he left the field. A second spectator attempted to tackle the Counties winger but witnesses said he bounced off. It was amusing to some but not to Lomu and the then Counties coach Mac McCallion admitted to the press: 'Jonah is worried by these attacks. When he is not being punched by idiots he is being accosted by screaming women. It's a serious matter and we are thinking of having the reserves form a flying squad which would escort Jonah from the ground and protect him. Although he can't have someone with him all the time, so I guess he'll have to deal with the screaming women himself.'

McCallion's flying squad plan never got off the ground, mainly because Jonah didn't want to punish the genuine fans who behave themselves. He actually admits to enjoying the feeling of being in demand, some of the time anyway. In this respect he hasn't changed much in terms of how he reacts to fame. 'I'm still the same person,' he insists, 'it's a good feeling to be admired by people. Having someone wanting your autograph or just saying hello is a great honour. It's a privilege to be admired and although it sometimes gets a little out of hand or too much to bear, I always try to make time to sign autographs, say hello to my fans and all that. You've got to keep control, breathe in some air, and give them what they want, within reason. I really mean it when I say it's an honour and a privilege. I couldn't change how I feel about that, despite the times when I've had to be escorted from the field or protected because of people who take advantage of the situation and lose control.'

While most of Lomu's admirers only want to congratulate and worship their hero, the Pukekohe attack was a warning of the dangers of success and fame. At one level, Jonah had arrived in sporting and social terms, proving that with determination and with 'God on your side' you can overcome almost anything, including semi-poverty and racial prejudice. And yet he risked, quite unintentionally, driving a wedge between himself and the world he had left behind, fuelling the jealousy of people who were not so long ago on the same economic and social level.

The tension surfaced again a few days after the Pukekohe incident. He was leaving a restaurant one evening when a group of three or four fans, slightly the worse for wear following a drinking session, jostled him slightly before asking for an autograph. Lomu turned and almost lost control, threatening to punch one of the men. Had he done so the consequences would have been painful for both. A punch from someone as powerful as Lomu would, nine times out of ten, require medical assistance and he would have undoubtedly been charged with assault. On another occasion an over-exuberant female fan accidentally caught Lomu with her nails, resulting in a nasty scratch on his neck. He was livid and had to be restrained.

The personal pressures that fame had begun to put on Lomu were mentioned by the player himself in a series of interviews. In one published shortly after the 1995 World Cup, only days after he turned down an offer of more than £2 million to switch to rugby league in England, when he was 20, he described the difficulties of making everyone happy – and meeting his contractual obligations – while keeping a sense of control over his own life. He spoke with warm pride about helping raise money for sick children, and his efforts to reply to letters from his fans and sign autographs. But he contrasted this with the people he claimed had begun to take advantage. 'Some of it is driving me crazy,' he said. 'Of course I'll help kids and sign autographs all day, but I can't be in three different places at the same time or say yes to all the promotions and obligations. Some people seem to have selfish reasons for wanting some of my time. I won't respond to that. I have a life outside rugby you know, but it's getting harder to do the things I used to do.'

The difference was that now Lomu could rarely do in secret what he had done since his late teens. A night out with his mates, taking in a movie, dancing at a club; all presented potential trouble in the form of unwelcome attention, sometimes from girls who wanted to score with the biggest draw in town, the kiss-and-tell tarts, and other times from guys hell bent on making a name for themselves. In an interview with a South African newspaper Lomu admitted: 'Sometimes it's safer to stay at home because there's always the tough guys around, you know, the ones who want to have a go at you. What do I say? I tell them, "Hey, I'm only human."'

In many respects marrying Tanya Rutter was the best thing that could have happened to Lomu. By all accounts the fame was getting to him and being of a somewhat passionate – some would say explosive – nature, it seems inevitable that sooner or later Lomu would have lost control, either resorting to violence to sort out the increasing number of jealous aggressors or succumbing to the seemingly endless parade of sex-for-fame girls on show for his eyes only. Either way, the media would have hung Lomu out to dry with the rest of the dirty washing and that would have been damaging at such an important stage of his fledgling career. While the attentions of obsessed females – real or imagined – were at this stage of his career and life the least serious of Lomu's concerns, maybe things would have turned out worse for him had he not turned a blind eye and declared undying love for the teenage South African. Lomu never played the rogue so that never became an issue, but what was beginning to trouble him was the fear of social displacement and threatened identity as he struggled to pursue his calling to rugby greatness amid the growing pressure of contractual and social obligations.

To play rugby and win remained, as it had from early teenage years, his key motivation. And yet his ability to perform had begun to be undermined by the emotional and mental instability caused by the very attention he had craved before he suddenly became a household name after the 1995 World Cup. Everything he had learned about self-control during his years at the disciplinarian Wesley College was slowly being eroded by the force of expectation and it was as though he was somehow regressing to the beginning of his teenage years when he had no self-control. Instead of walking away from trouble he started to think twice, hanging around for longer than he should as if to tempt fate. To an outsider his behaviour did not appear excessive, but his family and friends had seen the young Lomu go off the rails before and the warning signs were all too familiar; a destructive mood of arrogance and complete disregard for other people. Lomu was taking risks, pushing the limits of reasonable behaviour in his dangerously premature position as New Zealand rugby's most bankable asset. A week before the secret wedding he decided to take his tensions out behind the wheel of a high-powered sports car. Lomu makes no secret of his love for fast cars. 'They are a passion,' he said after taking delivery of a sponsored All Black Ford Hercules SVO in 1997. 'I've also got a BMW but what I really want is a Ferrari F50. I had a look at one when I was with the All Blacks in Italy. It's my dream car.'

With earnings of around $3 million a year from wages and sponsorship deals. Lomu will probably be able to afford the F50 by now. Lucky for him he didn't have access to one back in the New Zealand autumn of 1996. Then he had to make do with a borrowed Jaguar XJS but even so it had sufficient power to satisfy his appetite for risk-taking. The story goes that Lomu, at the time without a valid driving licence, hit speeds in excess of 200kph – 125mph – during what friends described as 'a complete blow-out' on roads in the mountain resort of Taranaki which lies in the west of the North Island on the Tasman Sea coast. According to one eyewitness, Lomu almost lost control of the car on a bad bend so it was probably a good thing that the Taranaki police turned up when they did. Lomu was caught driving at 127kph, fined $160 for speeding and $350 for driving without a licence; a small price to pay considering what the consequences could have been.

The incident, made worse by blanket media coverage, fuelled the anxiety in Lomu that he was no longer in control of his own life. Just like the reckless Jaguar ride, something was driving him faster than he knew he should be going. Suddenly he realized just how much he needed Tanya and that is why, when it came to the crunch, Jonah was prepared to put his parents through hell to make her his bride. In her he saw the answer to all his hopes and fears, even though, in the eyes of some of his friends, she was no more than a child.

To many outsiders, and others within the Lomu and Rutter family circles, the marriage was a mistake. 'They are both too young,' a close family friend of Tanya Rutter's parents told me. 'How will they cope? The pressures of a normal marriage are bad enough, but their relationship will be under even greater pressure because of Jonah's celebrity status. We are genuinely concerned for their well-being, but they are young and in love and believe they are doing the right thing. Only time will tell.'

14 THE WEDDING SINGER

**Maybe in this imperfect world,
only true love is perfect; maybe not.**

Anon

I t was an unusual act of romance, but as a measure of his love
and commitment to the girl he had married in secret Lomu's
insistence on carrying Tanya's wedding dress from Auckland
all the way to South Africa, via Hong Kong, hit the mark. Tanya
got the dress in America; it weighed over a stone – eight and
a half kilos – and Lomu's 40-inch arms were burning, slightly,
by the time they made it to Tanya's home town of Kimberley. In
fact it was so heavy that Tanya was forced to change within
hours of the ceremony because the weight of the dress was
making her uncomfortable. Her mother said she had never seen
a bride get out of her dress so early in the evening. Lomu
insisted on carrying it on the plane as cabin luggage, just in case
something happened. 'It was so heavy but he didn't complain
once,' Tanya Lomu told her friends before the wedding. 'I told
Jonah it would be okay sending it through with the rest of our
luggage but he insisted. The dress was everything I wanted and

he wanted to take care of it for me. It was a very romantic thing to do, but he's like that. A very romantic guy. It's one of the reasons why I love him so much.'

For Tanya Lomu, it was a strange homecoming. The controversy of the first wedding in South Auckland followed the couple from New Zealand to South Africa and threatened to overshadow the 'official' ceremony in Kimberley, and there was also the small matter of reuniting their respective families to deal with. While Tanya's parents publicly played down the disappointment of being kept in the dark about the first wedding, there was growing concern that behind the scenes the Rutters were far from happy about the situation. One South African newspaper suggested Alan Rutter wanted to call the whole thing off, such was his contempt for the way his daughter had embarrassed the family by agreeing to wed in secret. By all accounts Tanya had some tearful explaining to do before her parents finally accepted that the Kimberley ceremony must go ahead and that in time the humiliation and hurt caused by the young couple's insensitivity and haste would disappear. Besides, Tanya would be fulfilling a childhood promise to her mother, Maureen Rutter, by having a traditional white wedding at St Matthew's Anglican Church in her home town, even though the ceremony would be restricted to a renewing of vows. It was Maureen who organized most of the wedding; Hepi allegedly wanted no part of it at first, largely due to her anger at being excluded from the secret wedding.

The eyes of the world's media were watching and even Hepi and Semisi Lomu readily agreed to put on a brave face, although it would take more than the glitz and glamour of a big wedding in diamond country to heal the rift between them and Jonah. Not that the Rutters or Lomus were not looking forward to the Kimberley ceremony. They genuinely wanted peace and unity to bond their respective children in this 'official' union of marriage, it was just that wounded pride can take a long time to mend and both sets of parents were still coming to terms with the speed at which recent events had overwhelmed them. Jonah and Tanya knew this and went to great lengths to try and repair some of the damage caused by their decision to marry in secret. They were excited by the prospect of going through it all again, only this time with all the trimmings of a real high society event, but more than anything they were determined to make it a day for their parents to enjoy. Lomu was particularly looking forward to having his family around him on such an important occasion. This time they would all be present, his father Semisi, mother Hepi, baby sister Ailine and brother John, and Jonah booked their tickets in advance just to make sure.

As far as their own personal happiness was concerned Jonah and Tanya had no doubts at all that they were doing the right thing. True love doesn't always follow a golden path, and the hurt in the wake of the March wedding was a painful reminder of the pitfalls of the gravel road, but in their hearts the pair embraced new-found love. In the end nothing could prevent it from spilling out and covering, at least in part, the sins of South Auckland.

The joy of being Mrs Jonah Lomu was mentioned by Tanya herself in a candid but unpublished newspaper interview two days before the second wedding. In it she described the difficulty of pleasing everybody, especially Hepi and Semisi Lomu, and admitted that the decision to wed in secret had been a joint one. 'We always talk things through,' she said. 'We would not have gone through with it had one of us not been happy about it. We believe what we did was right. It will be with us for the rest of our lives but we can live with it. It might not have been the right thing in the eyes of everyone, and we did not enjoy upsetting our parents – that has been hard for us to deal with – but it is the way we wanted it. The first wedding was very special and the second one will be as well.'

Set in a semi-arid stretch of South Africa's interior, five hours from Johannesburg, Kimberley doesn't quite suit the title of diamond capital of the world. It took Lomu a while to appreciate its finer points, and at one stage the idea of a more exotic alternative, such as Tonga or Sun City, was mooted. There are some stunning buildings, like a rococo city hall and numerous ageing but opulent mansions, but Kimberley, when it comes right down to it, is a plain old mining town that just happens to pull carats from the ground instead of ore.

The city is the headquarters of the giant De Beers diamond organization, where diamonds mined locally, plus others mined in South Africa and Namibia, are sorted at the tall Harry Oppenheimer House which has the famous Digger Fountain in the Oppenheimer Memorial Gardens in front of it. Kimberley's mining operations have these days been dwarfed by diamond mines elsewhere on the subcontinent, so more emphasis is being placed on diversifying the mining-oriented industry and the area has been designated an industrial growth point. In terms of tourism, the Lomu wedding certainly represents a growth point in Kimberley's recent history, and the town will now always be equally associated with Jonah Lomu's name as with such pioneering men as Cecil John Rhodes, Alfred Beit, J. B. Robinson and Barney Barnato.

Residents of the South African town may disagree, but it's as though the giant star of world rugby suddenly blinded the world to Kimberley's rich past when he made up his mind to wed the daughter of a man who couldn't afford to buy a diamond before the Jonah Lomu show arrived in town. Put this theory to the test by calling the Kimberley tourist information service. Before they tell you about the diamonds and the Big Hole – a mining pit that is said to be the largest man-made crater in the world – and other gems such as the prehistoric rock carvings in Wildebeeskuil, 10km out of town, or the home of ANC founding father Sol Plaatje in Galeshewe, the oldest township in South Africa, or the five-star guest house where Nelson Mandela has stayed, they'll mention All Black legend Jonah Lomu and how he married his sweetheart, Kimberley's own homespun Tanya Rutter.

But although Kimberley's adopted son and the diamond mines are what it's best known for, there is much more to its history. Pivotal incidents of the Anglo-Boer War were played out here: the history of the Siege of Kimberley is brought alive in the McGregor Museum, a building which provided sanctuary to mining magnate Cecil Rhodes during the siege. The Magersfontein battlefield – where British troops trying to relieve the siege took a pounding from the Boers – is 40km out of town. The trenches are still visible from the hilltops and there is a museum next to the battlefield.

It is, when all is said and done, the capital of the Northern Cape, origin of the world's modern diamond industry, and Lomu himself wouldn't leave without taking a tour of the place where Kimberley started: the 'Big Hole'. Once a hill called Colesberg Kopje, situated in the wasteland north of the Orange River in the northern Cape, deposits of diamonds were found on the spot in 1870 and the discovery started one of the most frantic mineral rushes of the nineteenth century. The koppie was literally torn apart and it was found that the ground below was even richer in treasures which became, with years and years of feverish mining, the world's largest hand-dug excavation. In 1914 when the mine was closed, the hole had reached a depth of 1,097 metres and had yielded more than 3 tonnes – 14,504,375 carats – of diamonds.

At times there were up to 30,000 men working their kimberlite claims there. As the hole deepened, pathways that had criss-crossed the claims disappeared and open-cast mining developed. Kimberlite, or Blue Ground, is diamond-bearing rock which occurs in vertical 'pipes', sometimes as much as 2 kilometres in diameter, forced up from the earth's core about 80 million years ago. About 150 kimberlite pipes have been found in South Africa, but only 25 are diamond-bearing. Kimberley – a name derived from kimberlite – grew up around the mining activities at the best known of these kimberlite pipes.

The famous Star of South Africa diamond prompted Sir Richard Southey, the colonial secretary of the Cape, to declare: 'This is the rock on which the future success of South Africa will be built.' If it were not for the discovery of gold on the Witwatersrand, the prophecy would have come true. Nevertheless, Kimberley achieved many 'firsts': it housed the first stock exchange in South Africa, the first street lights in the southern hemisphere and the first flying school in Africa. Had Jonah and Tanya resisted the temptation to wed in secret, Kimberley would have played host to the first – the one and only – Jonah Lomu wedding.

Nevertheless, the fact that Auckland will go down in history as the place where the most feared winger in the history of the game first became a married man, failed to dampen the enthusiasm of the town's population. Officially there were 350 people at the wedding in Kimberley but unofficially there were about three and a half thousand. The Rutters' home town never knew what hit it; even Mandela would have struggled to pull in the crowds like Jonah and Tanya did. The place simply went wild and it has never been the same since.

There was a certain amount of clamour developing among the media to get to Tanya Lomu. All the big glossies were sounding her out for interviews, in part because Jonah was still proving difficult to talk to – mainly because of his often acute shyness. He wasn't comfortable giving interviews, especially if the interviewer probed too deeply into areas of his life he had yet to share with anyone except his close family. After all he was still only 20 and less than three years out of college, the confidence he showed on the rugby field conspicuous by its absence in other areas of his life. The World Cup had sprung Lomu into superstar status and the media were now describing him in such extravagant terms as 'the hottest property in world rugby' and 'potentially the greatest ever All Black'. But the often self-conscious Islander was not entirely at ease with the hype, so the media turned their attention to Tanya in the hope that she would shed some light on the hidden aspects of her new husband's character.

After the furore of the secret wedding on the banks of Manukau Harbour the New Zealand media headed for Kimberley in their droves. Together with overwhelming media interest in South Africa, as well as dozens and dozens of reporters from Britain, Europe, America, Australia and even Tonga, the diamond capital of the world was transformed into a media circus the like of which it had never seen before.

TVNZ's Paul Holmes and a team of producers from his show even went to Kimberley for a one-hour special on the wedding, reportedly paying a total of around $NZ30,000 for the privilege. Glossy women's magazine *New Idea* also paid for exclusive rights to the wedding – in excess of $NZ25,000. The joke among locals was: 'If the third world war starts this week, there'll be no one available to cover it.' Lomu had mixed feelings about the extent of the media coverage and he confessed to Tanya on more than one occasion that 'I wish they'd leave us alone.'

But that was never going to happen. In fact Lomu's reluctance to bare his soul to the world made the media even more determined to cover every aspect of his new life with Tanya, his career and his past. In the years that followed, as Lomu continued to shy away from interviews, stories about his ascent from semi-poverty to mega-riches became laced with exaggerations, untruths and downright lies.

There was nothing false about the revelations concerning his past relationships, although the timing was pretty lousy. Tanya already knew about Leanne Russell and Elaine Makiha, so the so-called 'exclusive' stories in various tabloid newspapers at the time did not take her by surprise. It was just their line of reasoning that caused the damage. When he returned to New Zealand after meeting Tanya at the 1995 World Cup, Lomu had ruthlessly split with Russell, his Auckland shop-girl fiancee, and moved into a new home with Tanya.

Although he was only 20 it was the second time he had broken an engagement. He had already dumped childhood sweetheart Makiha after a three-year romance, officially to devote himself to rugby. But there was someone else involved – Russell. Maybe it was sour grapes talking, but the girl Lomu promised to marry before he ever set eyes on Tanya Rutter had a point. 'How can you trust someone who goes from one relationship to another without so much as a care in the world?' she said. 'Jonah wears his heart on his sleeve, but it's so fickle. He is unstable and I doubt he'll ever change. Maybe one day he'll grow up, but he'll always be on the edge of some crisis or other.'

It was a genuine outpouring of emotion from a girl who gave her heart to Lomu only for him to cruelly break it. Maybe Tanya should have listened, but Russell's hurt was soon forgotten. Right now, the media were happy to let Tanya Lomu do the talking and she was happy to oblige, although she promised Jonah that conversations between him and his parents, especially his mother Hepi, resulting from the heartache and anger caused by the secret wedding, would remain taboo. 'That's between me and my parents and I want it to stay that way,' he said; and to a great extent it has.

In an interview with a reporter from South Africa's *Star* newspaper after the wedding, Tanya Lomu admitted: 'Jonah is quite a private man and although part of him really enjoyed having a big, glamorous wedding, because of all the support we had from family and friends, I think he was more at ease with the situation in Auckland when there were only a handful of people there. The wedding here was fantastic, a dream come true for me, but it was so overwhelming. I could not believe how many people turned up. They were sitting on the roofs of houses, on fences, on cars. I've never seen so many friends at one time.'

At least 40 guests came over from New Zealand, mainly family and friends of Hepi and Semisi Lomu, but also Jonah's All Black team-mate Michael Jones and Auckland Blues team-mate Charles Riechelmann, and manager Phil Kingsley-Jones.

But it was the Tongans who made the reception at Tanya's old school – Kimberley Girls' High – really swing. If Jonah's parents were still upset about being excluded from the first wedding they certainly didn't show it. 'They are a great bunch of people,' Alan Rutter said, 'there was lots of singing and dancing, at one stage there must have been 500 people on the dance floor doing the Macarena.' The wedding band was booked from 4 p.m. till midnight but they didn't leave until 7 a.m. Hepi Lomu wouldn't get off the microphone and sang through to the early hours with her husband Semisi on the keyboards, learning while he was playing. 'We left the reception at 5 a.m.,' Tanya recalled. 'Jonah and I ran a kind of ferry service in two cars for people who'd had alcohol. We took people all over town. Jonah booked tours around Africa for a lot of the guests from New Zealand. We got them to game parks, Cape Town and Sun City, and on the Sunday after the wedding we had a huge barbecue for everyone. We hired out a park, just for us. My parents had never been to New Zealand so it was time to get to know everyone. The families were meeting; getting to know each other. It was a special time.'

It was also an expensive time. The total cost to Jonah Lomu, who reportedly paid for most of the wedding, was a sizeable slice of his post-World Cup earnings. The whole event, including a honeymoon in the Virgin Islands and Disneyland, allegedly cost in excess of $NZ1.5 million – around £600,000 – although considering Lomu was turning down offers in the region of $NZ5 million from the United States and the UK following his success in the World Cup, he could afford to splash out. Anyway, as Tanya later told a New Zealand magazine, 'Jonah is the most generous man I know. He is completely unselfish.

'He is also very honest and we've got a really up-front relationship. If Jonah says something and I totally disagree with him, I'll tell him. If he's upset about something he comes to me straightaway. The same applies to me. That is what's made the relationship so good. We've built on it. We can be so open about anything.'

They met by accident or, in Jonah's own words, 'Fate brought us together.' It happened during the World Cup in South Africa, in Bloemfontein – a city of intense diversity on the road between Gauteng, KwaZulu-Natal and the Western Cape. Mangawung, the Tswana name for Bloemfontein, means 'place of the cheetahs' – a reminder of the wilderness which existed before farmers tamed the highveld plains where the city stands today.

Bloemfontein originated at a spring which at various times was a source of water for Bushman hunters, Sotho farmers, Voortrekkers and enormous herds of game. For a long time, it remained a tranquil agricultural settlement, but in recent years Bloemfontein has developed into a prosperous commercial and industrial city; the capital of the Free State and the judicial capital of South Africa. Monuments and museums testify to a pioneering past, and the opposing armies and innocent victims of the Anglo-Boer War. With its stately old buildings dominated by skyscrapers, the city has many facets, ranging from sophisticated up-market shopping centres, restaurants and theatres to vestiges of the gracious Victorian ambience which once prevailed. Surprisingly for a city that was formerly the capital of a Boer republic, Bloemfontein has many British features – legacies of the Anglo-Boer War when the town was occupied by British forces.

Both Jonah and Tanya had been invited to the same place for a barbecue dinner. It was a mistake because Lomu's future wife had no interest in rugby at all. In fact she didn't even know who Jonah Lomu was, yet in many respects it was love at first sight. 'I thought he was the most handsome man I had ever seen,' she recalls, 'and such a nice guy as well, shy but warm and very genuine. There was none of that "hey look at me, I'm a star" attitude. After we got to know each other a bit more, I realized just what a kind-hearted person he is. He really cares about other people and rarely puts himself first. That is important to me, especially because if I was going to leave my home and family and move to New Zealand with him, I needed to feel safe and secure with Jonah. But he made it easy to trust him, because of his sincerity.'

For several months after their honeymoon, during a settling-down period in South Auckland, being so far away from home was hard for Tanya. She was terribly homesick for her family and friends. For a while she had to speak to them every day to help her adjust to life in a new country and all the other difficulties of being the new wife of a man who had become New Zealand's number one personality. 'It was hard to uproot and move so far away from my home,' she added, 'but Jonah's made it easier for me; he's always around for me, and when he's away with the All Blacks he calls me as often as he can, sometimes several times a day, and he never stays away longer than is absolutely necessary. If you know somebody loves you and you've got solace, it's easier to cope with change. The unknown becomes less frightening.'

Love is a two-way street and at the time Jonah admitted he needed Tanya as much, if not more, than she needed him. Tanya was certainly the level-headed one in the marriage.

Jonah, by his own admission, is 'a dreamer' and a person who sometimes loses touch with reality, occasionally to the extent where his emotions take him for a ride. His heart often rules his head, although at the time Tanya insisted: 'It's not always a bad thing. It's just the way he is and I would not want to change that. We have a good understanding and Jonah is happy to let me make the decisions. He doesn't have a problem leaving things up to me.' In many ways it's a measure of Jonah Lomu's humbleness – some would say low self-esteem – that he allowed himself to depend so heavily on Tanya. She meant everything to him. Like anyone else, he has his demons and there is plenty of evidence to suggest that without the support of his wife and parents Lomu's life would still be more of a rollercoaster ride than a steady climb to the heights of superstardom. Not that he is emotionally retarded in any way; to the contrary he is as strong-willed and balanced an individual as you could hope to meet, but he knows his own limitations.

'I'm not afraid or ashamed to admit that I need Tanya more than anything else in my life,' he said shortly after celebrating their second wedding anniversary. 'She is more important to me than rugby, and I never thought I would feel that way. Rugby is my life but Tanya is more than life. The biggest and best thing in my world is having her by my side. That's what keeps me going. When things are bad that's important. It's about trust. Having someone I can turn to at night and say, "Honey, I really need some help," is so important. Tanya doesn't always agree with me, but that's part of the deal.'

Their private life was beautifully simple, and I doubt it would have changed very much if they had nothing. The things they liked doing are the simple things; talking, which they spent hours and hours doing, watching movies, going to the theatre, just walking together – late at night when the moon is full and bright and high over the Tasman Sea and the world is quiet but for the beating of their hearts.

Maybe, in this imperfect world, only true love is perfect. Maybe not. But one thing is clear; Jonah and Tanya Lomu had real happiness, at least for as long as it lasted. 'I've found someone I really love and really trust,' she told me in April 1998, shortly after their second wedding anniversary. 'We're not just married, we're best friends.' But fate was to play the cruellest of tricks on Tanya Lomu.

15 CHARGE AT THE ELEPHANTS

**We are all in the gutter,
but some of us are looking at the stars.**

Oscar Wilde

A way from the odd snatched moments of married bliss, Jonah Lomu was running all the time because he had so much going on. 1996 wasn't a particularly good year for him, largely due to injury problems and the strange tiredness that had hindered him since the beginning of the European tour to France and Italy towards the end of 1995, but he was still in demand as an international celebrity, newly wed husband and money-making machine. His playing schedule for the year would include the 1996 Hong Kong Sevens, several Test matches, the newly formed Tri-Nations series, and a hectic club programme with Counties Manukau. Tanya Lomu wasn't going to see much of her new husband, but she knew that before she married him and anyway, the money would be out of this world.

In early 1996 McDonalds and Reebok came knocking at Lomu's door, bearing lucrative sponsorship deals that would put the 20-year-old's earnings into the super-league. With Lomu now a household name, after making a lasting impression on more than 2.5 billion viewers who watched the 1995 World Cup, many of the largest and richest companies in the world were falling over themselves to marry their particular product with the No. 1 name in rugby union. Lomu signed a three-year contract with fast food giant McDonalds to promote its burgers, while Reebok secured his services on a four-year promotional deal for an undisclosed sum. In total, including his new contract with the New Zealand Rugby Football Union and their chief sponsor Steinlager, Lomu's earnings at that time were in excess of $NZ2 million a year. Suddenly he was a very rich man but, trying desperately to keep his feet on the ground and maintain some kind of vital balance in his life, Lomu once again began to feel the strain.

The first signs of this became visible as New Zealand commenced their quest for success at the Hong Kong Sevens tournament in March 1996 and continued to manifest, in various forms, as the year progressed. After winning the Hong Kong Sevens, during which Lomu had his moments but generally did not live up to expectations, New Zealand turned to All Black power to satisfy the country's ravenous appetite for rugby success. Lomu was to play in a series of five winter Test matches before a combination of physical and emotional wear and tear put a stop, albeit temporarily, to his playing career. The general feeling among close friends and family was that Jonah needed a break, or more importantly a breathing space. Apart from a short holiday with Tanya in northern Australia after the 1995 Bledisloe Cup triumph, it had been virtually non-stop rugby since the World Cup in South Africa. But calling time-out wasn't an option open to a man making huge sums of money from his reputation as an unstoppable force in the fast-changing world of international rugby. The people responsible for making him a multi-millionaire at the age of 20 would not allow him to stop; subdued but still unstoppable was barely acceptable, anything less would not do.

So, the weight of family pressures affecting his game and his body crying out for rest, Lomu began to walk a tightrope. Ironically, at such a young age and less than two years after making his All Black debut, he had already made enough money to retire. But at the top end of professional sport, the incentive to reach new heights and push towards the limits of endurance almost always overrides common sense and Lomu, fuelled with this desire to break new ground, made up his mind to press on. The blood disorder that had weakened him during the Test matches in Italy and France in October and November the previous year had not been properly diagnosed, let alone cured, and Lomu was also experiencing problems with his knees and groin. If his body was telling him to rest, Lomu should have listened, but he didn't and would later pay a heavy price.

He managed to find some of his World Cup form during the Tests against Western Samoa and Scotland in June 1996. Against the Samoans in Napier, Lomu impressed new All Black coach John Hart, who had replaced Laurie Mains after the 1995 European tour, with a workmanlike performance in a 51–10 victory. Seven days later in Dunedin, he scored a try and made two others as the All Black team crushed Scotland 62–31. There were flashes of his old brilliance but once again Lomu was more subdued than superior and Hart should have decided then to give him a rest. He didn't, and it wasn't until Lomu had almost collapsed after muscling his way through New Zealand's outstanding 43–6 victory over Australia in appalling weather conditions in Wellington on 6 July – the first professional rugby match between the two countries and the first match in the inaugural Tri-Nations series between the All Blacks, the Wallabies and the Springboks – that Hart finally realized Lomu's fitness levels were deteriorating.

But still, after further inconclusive blood tests and treatment for a niggling knee problem, Lomu persuaded Hart to allow him to continue. He played, although not especially well, in the 20 July Tri-Nations 15–11 win over South Africa in Christchurch, and occasionally made his presence felt in the close-fought Tri-Nations-Bledisloe Cup twin fixture against Australia in Brisbane a week later. The All Blacks won 32–25, their sixth consecutive win with Lomu on board since the defeat by France in Toulouse almost eight months earlier, but Lomu was not winning his fitness battle, not by a long chalk.

In the end, with his post-match recovery time worryingly high, Lomu was officially rested. He missed the Tri-Nations showdown against South Africa and it would be a month before Hart could select him again. When he eventually did, Lomu was still not 100 per cent fit. In gale force winds and driving rain, making handling and place-kicking almost a lottery and putting even greater physical demands on the players, the 21-year-old Lomu lasted the full 80 minutes of an All Black tour match against Eastern Province in Port Elizabeth, South Africa on 12 August. It was designed as a launch pad for Lomu to return to Test match rugby, but the expectant home crowd – more interested in Lomu than their own team, nicknamed the Elephants – were rewarded with only a fleeting glimpse of his raw power when Lomu swatted aside a couple of defenders en route to scoring his only try in an unconvincing 31–23 victory. Before the match Hart had optimistically put Lomu's chances of playing in the following Saturday's Test against South Africa at Durban's King's Park at around 90 per cent, but in reality they were nowhere near as high. Lomu had damaged knee ligaments and, more alarmingly, there was still something wrong with his blood.

There was no immediate way back this time and the problems that had started way back in October 1995 eventually cost Lomu the last six Tests of New Zealand's record-breaking run. In his absence the All Blacks completed a successful Tri-Nations campaign and recorded an historic first series victory in South Africa. Depressingly for Lomu, during his enforced break Jeff Wilson and Glen Osborne were in superlative form on their respective wings, and the harsh reality facing the world's most celebrated and highest-paid player as he convalesced at his South Auckland mansion, seeking solace in the arms of his concerned wife, was that he was scarcely missed. It was a time of mixed emotions; fame and fortune, but at what price?

Autumn turned to winter in New Zealand and good news for Lomu in September was overshadowed by more bad news towards the end of October. The player who, the previous month, had been honoured in a World XV selection – chosen from the best players of the past 25 years – landed himself in hot water with the New Zealand Rugby Football Union. Lomu, after being given the all clear to resume his playing by the All Black medical staff, was found guilty by a rugby union judicial hearing of a 'spear' tackle while playing for Counties in a provincial championship semi-final victory over Canterbury on Sunday 20 October 1996. The dangerous tackle earned him a one-week ban and caused a national controversy, especially after Lomu threatened to boycott the New Zealand Barbarians tour of England the following month. Lomu didn't carry out his threat because he knew the tour would provide the perfect stage for him to prove his fitness and once again underline his phenomenal ability, and more importantly his wife Tanya wanted to do her Christmas shopping in London. After months and months of feeling unwell, Lomu desperately wanted to be part of the Barbarians squad and he simply had to get away from Auckland, where the latest media ruck surrounding his 'spear' tackle was beginning to make him feel claustrophobic. England was definitely a Godsend.

As if transformed by a completely new environment, Lomu, with Tanya in tow, hit London with a sparkle in his eye. It was a startling contrast to the long-faced Lomu of Auckland who, during his enforced absence from the sport and subsequent troubled return, prowled around like a man facing a firing squad. Head down and sombre, he had been starved of fun, although there were moments when anonymity was both emotionally healing and blissful. In fact there were times when Lomu wondered if he might enjoy life without fame and fortune more than with it, but then he imagined life without rugby and the sadness returned.

But suddenly, in the middle of a savage cold snap, there was Lomu wearing a huge smile and a dazzling Hawaiian sweatshirt. Between Christmas shopping and sightseeing with Tanya, he laughed and joked and talked about his future and how he hoped to return to his best form as part of the New Zealand team to face England at Twickenham on Saturday 29 November – the difference a long-haul flight makes! The change was incredible, even more so when you consider that

Lomu had made the trip nursing yet another injury. This time a groin infection threatened to sideline him once again and ruin one of the most keenly awaited moments of the 1996 rugby season.

In an interview with the *Daily Telegraph* two days before the Twickenham match, Lomu admitted: 'It's been a really tough year but I feel the pressure is off now and that's been good for me. It's a huge challenge for me to get back into the New Zealand team. I still have a lot to prove, to myself and the New Zealand people. I can improve my game 100 per cent. I've got to get quicker and I can up my work rate. You have not seen the finished article yet.'

After an agonizing 24-hour wait, Lomu finally received the green light to take his place in the New Zealand Barbarians team. Despite having a quiet game by his usual explosive standards, he played well enough to create problems for England for most of the 80 minutes and made Carlos Spencer's try that tied up the match for the visitors. Lomu may have walked through periods of the game but the old threat was there as ever, unstoppable when he wanted to be.

It was an encouraging end to a difficult year and Lomu's heart was lifted as he and Tanya left the Christmas lights of London behind and headed back to New Zealand. They looked like a couple without a care in the world. But inside Jonah Lomu a time-bomb was silently ticking and there was nothing anyone could do to stop it. Within a few weeks it would bring him to his knees.

16 BREAKDOWN

I don't know the full details but being
diagnosed with nephrotic syndrome is
like being shot between the eyes if you're
a young athlete. It's an incurable
condition. You don't recover.

Dr Mike Turner, British sports medicine specialist

It was as though someone had killed the king, even though
there is no king; as though the sky had fallen in, even though
the summer sun still burned high over the land and sea.
Time stopped, even though Jonah Lomu counted the long
minutes, one by one, as they passed slowly by. He glanced at
his watch. He was waiting for a call. He needed to hear
Tanya's voice. Only she can ease my fear, he thought, and then
wondered if there was anyone else among the ghost-faces of
a shocked nation who had suffered or was suffering the same
fate as him. More than anything else he needed to hear Tanya's
gentle voice whisper: 'Don't worry baby, I'll protect you,' but
he also needed to hear someone, anyone, tell him that they had

beaten this terrible thing and that there was hope for him, even though he had already been told that there was little hope of a full recovery.

On the afternoon of Friday 24 January 1997, the news of Lomu's failing health hit New Zealand like a hurricane. Television and radio shows were interrupted, work stopped. Cities, towns and remote villages were quiet, people listened. They did not want to believe what they were hearing, but they had no choice. The truth hurts and right then, as a press conference revealed that the most feared winger in the game was seriously ill and might never play rugby again, a whole nation felt Jonah Lomu's pain.

There is no denying the severity of his condition, medical experts warned – the reality of the situation is that Lomu has been suffering from nephrotic syndrome for at least 18 months. He is very ill; his condition has worsened over the last three months and he now needs to have an intensive course of drug treatment. Could he die? someone asked, because at this moment only the doctors really understood what was happening inside the body of the once unstoppable All Black athlete, and even they were not entirely sure what was going to happen to Lomu. 'No, it's not fatal,' they replied, 'but he is suffering from a rare and incurable kidney disorder and has been told to stop playing indefinitely. The general prognosis is bleak, but not hopeless.'

Nephrotic syndrome is a condition marked by very high levels of protein in the urine; low levels of protein in the blood; swelling, especially around the eyes, feet and hands; and high cholesterol. It results from damage to the kidneys' glomeruli – the tiny blood vessels that filter waste and excess water from the blood and send them to the bladder as urine.

Nephrotic syndrome can occur with many diseases, including the kidney diseases caused by diabetes mellitus, but some causes are unknown, as in Lomu's tragic case. Prevention of the condition relies on controlling these diseases, although if you don't know what you are trying to control, treatment becomes something of a lottery. In most cases though, treatment focuses on identifying the underlying cause if possible, and reducing high cholesterol, blood pressure, and protein in urine through diet, medications or both.

Nephrotic syndrome may go away once the underlying cause, if known, has been treated. However, most of the time a kidney disease is the underlying cause, and these diseases cannot be cured. In such cases, the kidneys may gradually lose their ability to filter wastes and excess water from the blood. If kidney failure occurs, the patient will need dialysis or a kidney transplant. The possibility of death is remote, but not impossible.

Although tests during the 1996 season, when the All Black team was preparing to tour France and Italy, had revealed a minor blood disorder, nephrotic syndrome hit Lomu without warning and he knew nothing of it until the All Black team doctor John Mayhew pulled him off the field one training session to say further, more extensive blood tests were showing some abnormalities. Mayhew sent Lomu to see leading New Zealand kidney specialist Ian Simpson who recommended a six-month course of chemotherapy – corticosteroids and chloremucil – to treat his kidney disorder and stabilize his condition. It was not until Christmas 1996, after Jonah and Tanya had arrived home from England, that the full extent of the problem was officially diagnosed.

Both Simpson and Mayhew tried to remain positive. They did not want to panic a 22-year-old who could easily have been overwhelmed by such a frightening turn of events, but secretly they feared the worst. Simpson, who has seen many lives ruined by kidney disease, doubted Lomu could ever recover sufficiently to lead a normal life, and the hopeless prognosis of several other leading specialists, including the highly respected British sports medicine doctor Mike Turner, suggested that Simpson was right.

Unfortunately for Lomu and his devastated wife and family Turner's reaction to the news of the official diagnosis was picked up by the New Zealand press. Everything that Simpson and Mayhew, and to a lesser degree Hart, had done to ease the fears of a nation was shattered by the most shocking of analogies: 'Being diagnosed with nephrotic syndrome,' Turner suggested, 'is like being shot between the eyes if you are a young athlete. It's an incurable condition. You don't recover.'

Turner said that the best scenario was that Lomu's condition could stabilize, in which case he might still enjoy a relatively normal life. The worst scenario, Turner then admitted, was a gradual deterioration leading to kidney failure and the need for dialysis. Ultimately a kidney transplant might be necessary, using a close relative as a donor. Lomu's parents were distraught, in particular his mother Hepi who couldn't accept that normal healthy life for her son, let alone his rugby career, could be over. She called Mayhew who admitted: 'Maybe we should have found out earlier, but there was really no way of knowing. For the last 18 months Jonah has been sort of dragging a cart around, metaphorically. He's managed to train and play, I'm not sure how.'

'Will he be able to play again?' Hepi wanted to know, even though she was scared of the truth. 'Will he? Please tell me the truth.'

'I think so,' Mayhew replied, unconvincingly. 'He needs six months' rest, that's certain, but after that, we're not sure.'

'Oh,' Hepi whispered. 'I think I'd better speak to Jonah.'

Mother and son shed a few tears during the weeks that followed, and there were times when Lomu would suddenly wake in the middle of the night, fearful and confused. Those were the moments when he held Tanya tighter than ever, pulling her close, hiding his face in the warmth of her neck, seeking protection from the thing that threatened to destroy him.

February came and went and all the time Hepi prayed for her son. She got other people to pray as well, including Jonah whom she encouraged to 'have faith in God', and at such a desperate time of uncertainty, his own faith and personal beliefs became a great comfort and strength. 'I talked to God every day,' he recalled, 'and He helped me through.'

By mid-March Lomu's condition had improved, for the most part thanks to the specialist treatment he was receiving, but prayer had played its part as well. 'The best doctors in New Zealand, my family, my wife, and God are pulling me through,' he said at the time. Lomu was certainly feeling much better in himself, even though he was far from cured, and his relaxed and smiling face said it all as he spent a day commentating for ITV on the Rugby World Cup Sevens at the Hong Kong Stadium, the arena where his remarkable talent was first unveiled before an unsuspecting rugby world in 1994. 'I'm still playing a waiting game,' he admitted, 'but I'm feeling fit and I am just bursting to get out there again.'

He was three months into a six-month course of steroids designed to combat nephrotic syndrome but his next declaration, that 'if I wanted to play now I could', was far from the truth. He would certainly have failed any random drug tests because of the steroids, but more importantly he was still quite poorly. The treatment had weakened his immune system, increasing the risk of picking up infections. It would be another five months before he would be well enough to return to the training field, let alone play a competitive game of rugby.

On 6 August 1997, less than three months after his 22nd birthday, Lomu was cleared to resume graduated training. He had completed the six-month course of chemotherapy and his condition had been officially stabilized. Simpson and Mayhew, both of whom supervised the treatment, reached the decision after seeing Lomu in Auckland the previous evening. They were pleased with his medical status and general physical condition and immediately ordered a fitness assessment by the All Black coaching staff, under Mayhew's supervision. Coach John Hart then announced to the media that within a week a structured fitness programme to facilitate Lomu's return to rugby would be prescribed, although this would be closely monitored and no precise date for playing had been decided.

'Jonah will need to remain on medical treatment to maintain and consolidate his improved kidney function,' Mayhew explained. 'None of the medication should adversely affect his physical performance or contravene the drug testing regulations. But let's not get ahead of ourselves. We're taking no chances with him.'

At the end of August, following stage one of the structured fitness programme, Lomu made tentative plans to play for 40 minutes in a low key non-competitive friendly, only to withdraw, and less than two weeks later, on 11 September, the NZRFU medical experts ordered him to cancel similar plans for the following weekend. Lomu took it badly. At the Hong Kong Sevens, five months earlier, he had talked confidently about playing again for Counties in the New Zealand Provincial championships by the end of July. Now, at this rate, it looked as though he would not play again before 1998, and that would mean missing the New Zealand tour of Britain in November and December.

'I haven't played in almost 12 months,' he said, recalling his last game when he turned out for the New Zealand Barbarians against England at Twickenham. 'What's going on? I'm going crazy!'

The question was directed at All Black team physiotherapist David Abercrombie who, together with Mayhew and fitness expert Martin Toomey, decided to put Lomu through a series of new tests on Thursday 11 September to assess strength, stamina, and speed. The results spoke for themselves.

'You are not ready to play again,' Abercrombie told Lomu. 'Your fitness is improving but it's still not good enough. You'll just have to be patient.'

Lomu felt like exploding. He felt as though he could 'tear through' 80 minutes of Test match rugby, never mind a 40-minute friendly. 'I was frustrated,' he recalls, 'but there was nothing I could do. After almost 12 months without a game I was going nuts, but still they wouldn't let me play.'

Mayhew's statement to the New Zealand press after the 11 September tests was: 'Jonah is making fair progress and he may pass a similar programme next week. Generally, he is looking fairly good. Some of that puffiness caused by the treatment has gone and he is very enthusiastic about getting back to play rugby. He is not ready yet, but he is over the worst and it can only get better for him from now on.'

The transformation had not been without its trials. At one stage Lomu was taking up to 12 tablets a day. As a side-effect his appetite raged and his weight ballooned. 'I think my darkest moment was eating two chickens a day,' he said. 'What really scared me was when I jumped on the scales and was about 148 kilograms, and I said 'Doc, what's going on here?' It was from the treatment. But the next month the weight sort of dropped off me. The treatment has definitely been the toughest part. It knocks you about, gives you headaches and colds, tiredness. It wipes you out.'

As for Simpson, he was at last beginning to look on the bright side. As he prepared to relaunch his career Lomu asked him how good were his kidneys out of ten, and Simpson gave him a seven. Lomu was pleased about that, 'because it was only supposed to be 50-50 that the illness would look after itself,' he said. 'It can sometimes be put into remission, as appears to be happening with me, but it can also return unexpectedly. I'm not going to dwell on that, though. I'm staying positive. I believe I've got it licked.'

17 ONE SMALL STEP

**Inspiration, that's what he is;
inspiration to battle against the odds,
inspiration to never give up. Jonah's a
tough guy all right, tough on the inside;
where it counts.**

Sean Fitzpatrick

It was at a dinner to raise money for the Sir Richard Hadlee Sports Trust in Christchurch in mid-October 1997 that the news of Lomu's inclusion in the All Black squad for the November tour to Britain first leaked out. Coach John Hart wanted to keep it under wraps for another week, at least until the official unveiling of his 36-strong squad on 12 October, but by the time the Hadlee dinner had ended, Hart's best kept secret was out in the open. The result was a scrambled face-saving exercise by the NZRFU, who issued a warning to all New Zealand players to ignore any rumours about the content of the All Black squad until Hart himself had finalized the list.

Of course the rumours were true. Lomu had already proved his fitness, after many false starts, and only a cruel twist of fate, such as a relapse or injury, could keep him from joining the rest of the All Black team for the long trip west to Britain. Lomu finally ventured out on to a football field, for the first time in ten months, at the end of September in a reserve grade match for his province Counties and then the following day as a surprise inclusion in the second half of Counties Manukau's National Provincial Championship win over Otago. He could not have asked for more than Counties going to a 16–14 win, with Lomu himself contributing two tries. Less than two weeks later, on 12 October, he marked his full return to provincial rugby with two further tries in Counties' 85–17 win over Southland.

Hart had seen enough. Lomu was definitely fit enough to be included in the All Black squad and he wasted little time in informing the 22-year-old. Lomu recalls: 'I got told after our game at about 6.30 p.m. that John Hart wanted to speak to me. I thought it is either good news or bad news and I prepared myself for the worst.'

His gut instinct lied. It was good news, and Lomu was so excited by his return to international rugby that he could not sleep at all the night after he was told by Hart he had made the team. He kept thinking about the bleak prognosis of the medical experts who, nine months earlier, clinically said that he had only a 50-50 chance at best of making his way back to playing rugby at all. If through chemotherapy and pills he could not recover to the point where he could play rugby 'without the danger of damaging his enlarged kidneys', then that would be that, and rugby would simply never see Lomu again.

And yet, thanks to modern medicine, a small miracle and a slice of good fortune, here he was; back in black and ready to rumble, although in a candid interview with the *New Zealand Herald* the day after Hart broke the good news to him, Lomu admitted: 'It is scary playing again. I didn't know what to expect because I'd been out for so long, but I feel comfortable now that I've got the first one under the belt.'

So too did Hart and the NZRFU selectors, because they were counting on Lomu emerging as the All Blacks' main strike weapon, just as he had been before he was struck down by nephrotic syndrome. While Hart, to his credit, tried to lower expectations, it was still an unfair and unrealistic target for a young man whose playing weight was around 18 stone, who had only months earlier ballooned to an unbelievable 23 stone plus, largely through a heavy course of pills, and was still some way short of full Test match fitness. To return to the kind of devastating form that saw him score four tries with only seven touches of the ball during the 1995 World Cup semi-final thrashing of England, was a bridge too far for Lomu.

Hart knew it and so did Lomu. 'After having a long chat with him, it's pretty clear that there is a need to be realistic about his current physical condition,' said the All Black coach. 'It would be easy to get carried away and expect Jonah to walk back into the side and pick up where he left off last year. But that won't happen because he is still not 100 per cent and he's only had the one full game, although that was pretty devastating. And besides there is a mental adjustment that has to take place, as well as the physical adjustment of returning to international rugby. I'm not expecting great things from Jonah on the tour. He is here for the future. He is a remarkable individual just to be in the squad, because it takes a special kind of person, someone with courage and character, to come through all that he has suffered and get back to playing rugby in less than 12 months.'

But while Hart was pushing the line that 'he is probably a better person for what he's been through and it could also make him a better player', Lomu was facing up, with a certain amount of anxiety, to the mental adjustments required to switch back into All Black mode. Knowing the challenges that lay ahead, he admitted: 'Returning to the All Black team would be like running on to the field for the very first time again. You get the butterflies and other things, like spewing in the corner. I've virtually jumped in the deep end.'

Fortunately for Lomu he is a strong swimmer; something he learned as a young boy, metaphorically swimming against the tide of his troubled past as he learned how to play the game at Wesley College. Then the changing current of life threatened to drag him under on more than one occasion. And no sooner had he returned to the familiar, and relatively calmer, waters of All Black rugby than the tide changed again and threatened to drown his hopes of playing on the British tour.

Five days after watching his Counties team-mates hammered 44–13 by Canterbury in the final of the National Provincial Championship in Christchurch, Lomu suffered a much worse setback when a change of medication for his kidney problem adversely affected his form at All Black training. In his vital preparation for the tour after the squad assembled in Auckland during the last week of October, Lomu failed to complete a three-kilometre time trial. For a moment, it looked as though Hart might pull him out, but following a meeting with team doctor John Mayhew, it was agreed that a change in medication was largely to blame, and Lomu's overall fitness, notably his stamina, would improve once his body had adjusted.

It was a good judgement call, especially on the part of Mayhew. He must have been the most relieved and satisfied man in Wales, with the exception of Lomu, when the young winger started his first match in an All Black jersey in over 15 months at Sardis Road, Pontypridd on 9 November 1997. It was his first significant comeback, an acid test, and he came through with flying colours, albeit with little help from Wales A who were not about to give way too easily to sentiment.

They targeted him from the start. He was scragged and jabbed from the kick-off until it became less easy to keep him down. Despite running on less than 80 per cent capacity, there was enough bulldozing power in much of his running to scare the living daylights out of the Welshmen who initially had the audacity to give him a hard time on his long-awaited come-back. In the last quarter Lomu stepped up a gear, to test his power, pace and stamina, and created familiar havoc among the defence with his front-on freight-train running. His hard work was rewarded with a try in the 66th minute, contributing to an emphatic 55–8 victory for the All Black team.

There was no doubt now, Jonah Lomu was back, and in achieving what many believed would be impossible following the onset of nephrotic syndrome, he had unknowingly fulfilled the prediction of one of rugby's greatest thinkers, South African coach Kitch Christie.

It was the morning after South Africa had won the 1995 World Cup. Christie had done an overnight flit to his remote game farm in the bushveld, alone with his family and his memories. He was dying from cancer, but strangely happy. His beloved team were champions of the world and he had witnessed the birth of a rugby legend, Jonah Lomu. Despite the controversy over the All Black team's food poisoning and subsequent bitter defeat to South Africa in the final, Christie's spirit lifted every time he thought about Lomu, and how the young New Zealand winger had lit up the tournament with his unstoppable pace and power.

Christie, born in Johannesburg but educated at Leith Academy, Edinburgh, came late to coaching but he took what had been an under-achieving squad, long on tradition and potential but short on harmony, direction, desire and self-belief, and made them into world champions. Christie became South Africa's most successful coach with 14 wins in 14 matches. Unassuming and reserved, he became part of the beautiful myth of the rainbow nation. The victory on home soil in 1995 touched people far beyond rugby's normal constituency. Nelson Mandela, wearing the captain's No. 6 shirt, embraced Pienaar after South Africa's 15–12 extra-time win over New Zealand.

Christie wasn't interested in politics though. That's why, as he sat with his family on the night of South Africa's World Cup triumph, he talked only of rugby and how it had transformed his life. 'I like that boy Lomu,' he said. 'What a great young player, what a character. I think he's got a big future in the game, and boy, did he put the wind up our guys. They didn't know what to make of him.'

Joel Stransky, whose dramatic dropped goal won that final for South Africa, said: 'I remember sitting alongside Kitch, watching the All Blacks demolish England in the semi-final on TV. At the end he shook his head. He was a worried man. But Kitch sat there and re-ran the tape. Again and again. Then he stood up and said simply: "We can beat them." And we believed him. Kitch was a great man. He was honest and direct but also warm, which is why we all loved him so much. It really was a special time in all our lives. His bravery was immense. I'd love to be able to lead my life like him.'

Christie was never fazed by hype. Everyone was worked up about stopping Jonah Lomu in that final. Not Christie. He just wanted to work on scrumming the All Blacks into the ground. He was not demonstrative but he had deep feelings. He was a decent South African who became a hero. He was first diagnosed as having lymph cancer in 1979 and he bore his illness with fortitude, but the disease took its toll on him and he died at the age of 58 in April 1998.

But before rugby lost one of its greatest treasures, Christie once again turned his thoughts to the player who had made him tingle with excitement during the last World Cup. By now Lomu was out of the game, battling to overcome nephrotic syndrome. Christie felt for the stricken All Black, especially as his own illness was nearing its awful conclusion, but he insisted: 'That boy won't quit and the illness that is threatening to end his career won't win. Don't ask me why, but there's something about him that says he will last. I've just got a feeling that the world hasn't seen the last of Jonah Lomu.'

Christie was proved right, although by the time Lomu returned to international rugby the South African was too ill to share in the worldwide appreciation of the young All Black star's wonderful achievement. At least he was spared the sight of seeing Lomu's life take another turn for the worse. 'Good things never last,' the wise old South African remarked to one of the doctors treating him at a New York clinic during the last days of his life, and Lomu was about to find out the hard way that fate is not always fair in its distribution of good fortune and bad luck.

18 END OF INNOCENCE

The bigger they come, the harder they fall.

Robert Fitzsimmons

A t least Kitch Christie had the satisfaction of knowing that Lomu had proved the medical experts wrong, just as he had proved his own doctors wrong in surviving cancer for almost 20 years. Maybe Lomu will survive nephrotic syndrome for even longer, maybe not, but at least one thing is certain, Christie wasn't around to say 'I told you so,' when the rollercoaster ride that is Lomu's career and life took another bad twist and heart-stopping dip in the New Zealand spring of 1998, resulting in another health scare and the break-up of his short marriage to Tanya. Good things never last, or at least they don't if you don't want them to.

For Lomu, married life lost its appeal, his relationship with Tanya lost its romance, and even the game of rugby ceased to satisfy the deep, overwhelming emotional needs of a man who may never completely get rid of the demons in his life. Maybe it was the silent, terrifying screams of fear in his soul that signalled the beginning of the end of the life that he had made with Tanya. Lomu was running scared again because there are signs that he may not have 'licked' nephrotic syndrome after all. After playing a starring role in helping New Zealand Sevens win gold at the Commonwealth Games in September, Lomu's condition deteriorated. He felt sick, desperately tired, and, at times found himself in great pain as his body struggled to cope with the sudden onslaught. His already damaged and enlarged kidneys were reacting to the punishing workload of the previous three months and, although his condition quickly stabilized again, the experience sent Lomu into an emotional and mental spin.

The sad irony is that Tanya, who nursed him through the worst times of his crippling illness, ended up paying the price. Lomu, showing all the signs of the desperation, frustration, and destructive urges that sent him off the rails before in his life, decided to terminate the marriage. He didn't even bother to tell Tanya, choosing instead to have a few days' holiday in Kuala Lumpur and Singapore before returning to New Zealand and moving in to a friend's apartment in Auckland. He walked out of Tanya's life without even saying goodbye, three weeks short of her 22nd birthday, and within days lawyers were called in to begin divorce proceedings. I spoke to Tanya at the beginning of October. She was all alone at the Italian-style mansion Jonah had bought for them before their moonlit wedding on the banks of Manukau Harbour in March 1996. I phoned to speak to Jonah about this book, but he had already gone, speeding off one night in his Ford Falcon, his belongings already in someone else's home, collected by a friend a few days earlier.

'He's gone,' Tanya said, her voice quiet and sad. 'Jonah's left me and he's not coming back.'

That was all she said, all she wanted to say, and my heart sank, not only because I felt the pain of a genuinely warm, caring, and deeply special woman, but also because I feared for Jonah. It was Tanya who prevented him from throwing it all away when the pressures of stardom threatened to crush him, and it was Tanya who encouraged, comforted, and bullied him through his torment when he contracted nephrotic syndrome. But that obviously wasn't enough for Lomu, and even more worrying was the news that, for the first time in his career, he had started to neglect rugby as well; his special love that held pride of place above everything else in his life.

He failed to turn up for training at Steelers Stadium, home of his club side Counties, at the end of September and then missed an end-of-season photoshoot a few weeks later. Even more disturbing was the news that he was once again threatening to walk away from the game forever. I suddenly remembered the words of Leanne Russell, the shop-girl fiancee who Lomu ditched for Tanya after the 1995 World Cup. 'Jonah is unstable and I doubt he'll ever change. Maybe one day he'll grow up, but he'll always be on the edge of some crisis or other.'

In the early hours of a cold morning in mid-October 1998, after three days of unsuccessful phone calls to New Zealand, I finally got to speak to Lomu himself. He'd been missing for some time but insisted: 'I'm getting things sorted, in my head.' They sounded like the words of a man who wasn't sure about anything any more. They were hollow and reverberated with confusion.

'What about Tanya?' I asked.

'We're history,' he said sharply, 'what else?'

'Rugby,' I replied. 'What about your career? What are you planning to do?'

'Hey,' he said, 'that's my business. I love rugby, but right now I've got a lot of thinking to do, about a lot of things.'

He hung up, leaving me and the rest of the world on the edge of our seats. What will happen to Lomu next? I wondered, daring to believe that this is not the end of the most feared winger in the game. I hoped he and Tanya might patch things up, but it seemed unlikely. More than anything else, though, I hoped Tanya, at least, would find her own happiness. And that Jonah Lomu, in all his confusion, would pack up his troubles and head for the 1999 World Cup with the same energy and hunger and explosive pace and power that had us all shouting for more when he hit South Africa like a hurricane those few years ago. He may have an incurable illness and he may be a loose cannon but the boy can play. Oh yeah, the boy can certainly play.